NEVER GET A TATTOO

Also by the author

TAMING YOUR GREMLIN

NEVER GET A TATTOO

Simple Advice on the Art of Enjoying Yourself

RICHARD D. CARSON

illustrations by Novle Rogers

PERENNIAL LIBRARY

Harper & Row, Publishers, New York
Grand Rapids, Philadelphia, St. Louis, San Francisco
London, Singapore, Sydney, Tokyo, Toronto

First PERENNIAL LIBRARY edition published 1990.

Designed by Alma Orenstein

Library of Congress Cataloging-in-Publication Data

Carson, Richard David.
  Never get a tattoo / Richard D. Carson.—1st Perennial Library ed.
    p.   cm.
  ISBN 0-06-096509-6
  1. Happiness.   2. Conduct of life.   I. Title.
BF575.H27C378   1990
158′.1—dc20   89-46080

90 91 92 93 94 CC/MPC 10 9 8 7 6 5 4 3 2 1

To Leti with love

CONTENTS

	Acknowledgments	ix
1	Never Get a Tattoo	1
2	True Love	6
3	Your Gremlin	9
4	Choose to Be Here	12
5	The Natural You	14
6	Make Enjoying Yourself a Top Priority	16
7	Clearly Experience Where You End and All Else Begins	20
8	Observe Your Props and Players	25
9	Breathe, Dammit, Breathe!	30
10	If You Can't Run with the Big Dogs, Keep Your Ass on the Porch	38
11	Relax Your Pact to Keep Your Act Intact	44
12	Resolve Conflict: Observe Your Feelings	48
13	Resolve Conflict: Face Your Foes	57
14	Change with Change	63
15	Release Your Outdated Concepts	72
16	Simply Notice and Play with Options	78
17	Just Imagine It [Redesigning]	86

18 Plan and Do   92

19 Re-Experiencing   95

20 Set Your Internal Metronome   102

21 Let Up Without Letting Yourself Down   105

22 Reminisce   108

23 Fall into Love   116

24 Do Service   122

25 Tune and Tone Your Solo Instrument   128

26 Hang Out   131

27 Wear Your Clothes   136

28 Mourn Your Losses   140

29 A Final Word   143

ACKNOWLEDGMENTS

My life has been graced by a steady stream of extraordinary souls in ordinary clothes. Take my wife Leti and our son Jonah, for instance. The privilege of sauntering through life arm-in-arm with those two buckaroos is a gift like no other. To them and to whoever arranged it, I owe a "thanks" way too big for the word. And there's my friend and assistant Mary Jurin Sonkin. I appreciate the way Mary takes my work seriously and me with a grain of salt. It's a hard line to walk sometimes. And thanks to my fleet-footed, eagle-eyed friend Phil Eagleton. He ran roughshod over my rough draft, and while he was hard on my work, he was gracious to my ego.

This is a clearer work because of the editorial suggestions of Daniel Bial at Harper & Row, and I am indebted to Dan. Thanks, too, to Irv Levey for his straight talk and encouragement early on in this project. To Novle Rogers, whose illustrations embellish this work, I offer a West Texas, buddy-to-buddy sock on the arm. His art's got heart. And Harry Clemens also has my appreciation. He's not much at racquetball but he's a prince of a fella. Chapter 1 makes clear his contribution to the happening you're holding.

I've had some splendid teachers and want to thank at least a few of them here. First and foremost is Maharaji. His effect on me seems boundless and I feel a deep love and gratitude for his knowledge and guidance. I'm grateful, too, to my mother and friend, Eva Segal Carson, a light of love and wisdom who sees life for what it is and has never been afraid to look it squarely and lovingly in the eye and then ask it to dance.

For three years in the early seventies I found myself in the midst of a group of uniquely talented facilitators at a place in time called the Gestalt Institute of Chicago. I learned a great deal from them all and feel a special debt of gratitude to Claire Ridker and Charlotte Rosner. Their commitment to authenticity and to openly sharing their experience inspired me to share my own.

Love to all of them and to you for coming along for the ride.

1

NEVER GET A TATTOO

Still sweaty and stiff from our racquetball game, Harry and I sat outside my house in his shiny new long and lean Lincoln Town Car. This morning's skirmish for the top of the athletic heap had been especially intense—the consummate competitive encounter, demanding of each combatant a honed mind and a toned body. The court was our battlefield. We were men, real men, just like in the television commercials. Skin glistening with perspiration, headbands, Nikes—only shorter, and balder, and a little older, maybe. But what the hell, we were males. The hairy sex—virile, courageous, congenial, intellectual. Brethren (albeit in the broadest sense), or distant cousins maybe, of the big names: Abraham, Isaac, Elvis.

Harry had beaten me two out of three games. In the locker room, I'd belted out "good game" and given him a swat on the back. It was a confident "who cares, it's only a game, it's the exercise that counts" kind of swat. I had adorned it with a casual whistle—"Old Man River," I think, or "Teddy Bears' Picnic." I caught a glimpse of myself in the mirror, a strained smile hardly masking the fire flashing in my eyes. There I was, whistling and swatting, all the while having rapid-fire fantasies of bashing Harry's face in with my racket, the side of my racket, the hard part. How could I be such a phony? It was easy. I

1

hate to lose. At times like these I covet my right to be petty and small. I wasn't about to crawl out of my rathole—not yet. I gotta be me.

The five-minute ride to my house was a quiet one— but for my whistling. His shiny new ride parked at my curb, there we sat—me brooding, Harry gloating.

We lit up a couple of hand-rolled Macanudos. It was a ritual we had repeated almost weekly for years: the game, the ride, the cigar, the sweat, and the swat. But this morning was unique—not just because Harry had out-scored me, but because it was the morning of my fortieth birthday. My fortieth birthday and he'd wiped up the court with me. My fortieth birthday and he was driving the new car. Here we were, straddlin' the seesaw of life, his head getting warmed by the sun and me so weighted down with a wet cloak of the beady-eyed, tiny-mouthed, touch-me-I'll-bite blues that I could barely see any light at all. Worse yet, Harry had turned forty on March thirty-first and had thirty full days of life experience on me. There I sat, the green kid cowering in the shadow of the confi-dent old pro. I wanted to bite a chunk out of his leg. I wanted to bring him to his knees. I wanted him down in the junkyard with me. But I played it cool. I stopped whistling long enough to stretch real big and faked a casual "lah-de-dah, life's just a bowl of cherries" yawn. I ended the yawn with, "So . . ." As in, "So, it's been a slice."

"So what?" he asked. Seemingly innocent verbiage I know, but I wasn't fooled for a minute. Subtle though it was, I spotted the self-glorifying weasel's veiled arro-gance.

It was just like in racquetball. The momentum was on Harry's side of the car. His confidence was up, mine was down. He felt big and proud. I felt shriveled-up and mean.

I waited for an opening and then I hurled the gaunt-let.

"So, big fella, you're older and wiser. Lay some

2

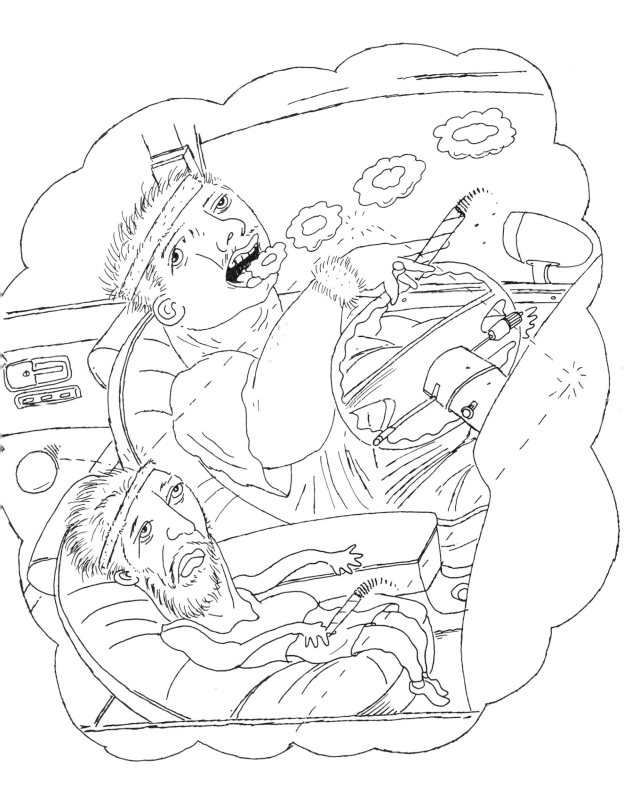

wisdom on me. Give me some advice on turning forty."
I felt it. The "best man" momentum shifted slightly to my side of the car. The gauntlet was on his side. Harry paused. His upper lip twitched slightly. He wanted to stay smooth but I'd broken his stride with my deft delivery. Pumped with the confidence of his win, Harry snatched up that gauntlet, leaned back in his broad leather Lincoln seat, took a pull on that big see-gar, and let go of a smoke ring that would have made the Great Gildersleeve green with envy. It was his day. The momentum was again in his favor. My mouth got dry. I braced myself. Then he looked at me steely eyed, and with the unflinching confidence of the Lone Ranger, he laid it on me. "Never get a tattoo," he said.

The words went straight to my heart. I'm no Spinoza, but I knows the truth when I hears it. I blew a pretty fair smoke ring of my own and nodded thanks.

I'm a solid forty-five now, I've not gotten a tattoo, and my life since that morning over five years ago has been upwards of fine and dandy. I believe in sharing a good thing, so I'm passing Harry's tidbit of universal wisdom on to you. It's sound advice. It says something about the trap of having permanently inscribed on your arm, your hip, or your psyche, for that matter, a concept of who you are or who you imagine you're supposed to be; something about being careful about what you advertise; something about the myth of unalterable truths; and more. But I liked Harry's advice before my mind had made a lick of sense out of it. That's how it is with good advice.

There's good advice and bad advice, but the kind of advice I like the best hits you smack-dab between your eyes, skitters past your brain before you can make sense of it, and nestles somewhere behind your heart, from whence it reminds you, ever so subtly, of who you really are. Often it comes from seemingly unlikely sources. It doesn't have to be agreed with, disagreed with, or understood—just experienced. It's simple. It's practical. It's offered in the spirit of friendship (even if its giver and receiver have never met face-to-face). It strikes a chord of common experience and it resonates with common sense.

You're holding a book of advice. Sound advice, offered in the service of a central theme: enjoyment of this precious and wonderful life. I myself am the beneficiary of vast amounts of helpful advice, probably because I have many special people in my life. People like Harry, with whom I am both teacher and learner—more the latter than the former, it seems, though I rarely admit it. Some pay me to help them get the most from their lives, and although I don't like to think it's so, I fear that if they know how much I learn from them, it will upset the apple cart, they'll stop paying me, and I'll have to get a real job.

Putting this fact in writing is a little scary for me. My generation calls this sort of daring openness ''risk taking.'' In Czarist Russia, my father's generation called ''fleeing the Pale'' risk taking. How one sees risk taking, like how one sees love, war, oneself, and every other person, place, and thing in the universe, is a matter of opinion. What follows is my opinion. It is based on experience, however, and it is as true to that experience as I can possibly make it.

By far the most important aspect of my experience, and of yours whether you are ready to acknowledge it or not, is love—true love.

2

TRUE LOVE

Don't gag and don't slam this book closed. I'm not about to embark on some schmaltzy speech laden with images of rainbows or doves or little round yellow happy faces. The love I am speaking of is far more incredible, far more beautiful, and far more powerful than any of those symbols imply. You have some of it in your life, but you want much more. You will work for it, fight for it, lie for it, give it to get it, and if you're honest with yourself, you will, at some point, acknowledge that you are devoting your entire life to filling yourself up with it.

It's always been important to you, but now that you're a grown-up it's high time that you wake up and acknowledge the prominence of your quest for true love as an influence and as a motivator in everything you do. It will make your life simpler and you a lot happier. In fact, you can be happy as a hoot owl from here on out; and that's an audaciously bold statement when you consider that at this moment, if you're over thirty, your skin is getting looser, your ears are getting bigger, your nose is getting longer, and the distance from the bottom of your feet to the top of your head is shrinking. Woe is you. But you're okay. Better than okay. Trust me.

Reflect on this: You. Yes, you, the one whose eyes are following these words. You are completely capable of enjoying this life much more than you ever dreamed possible, and it's easy. "Easy?" you say. "Why, I oughta . . ."

Well, hold on and listen up. The love you want and the love you have the capability to find is richer and more vibrant than anything you've ever imagined. It is, in fact, completely uncontaminated by your imaginings (or mine) about it. It is real. It is pure. Think of that—pure love—a limitless, rich, vibrant stash of pure love, and it's not love *of* anything. It's just flat-out love, and it is stirring inside of your body at this very moment. It comes with being alive. It is a gift. Just as the sun shines constantly whether you can see it or not, this love flows within your body whether you are aware of it or not. And you don't have to be religious, a yogi, a swami, an avatar, an advanced soul, or even a cool cat in order to experience it.

I double-dog dare you to consider that what I'm telling you is the truth; that you can be happier than you ever dreamed possible. And to become so, all you have to do is patch into that batch of true love that is already humming away inside of you. In fact, you would already be a blue-ribbon lover were it not for a pesky critter with which you must contend—a pest who, like true love, exists within you. He's a vile and vicious bully and his intention is to divert you from the love within and to ultimately destroy you. That's right, vile and vicious—not to mention powerful, ominous, and downright nasty. Let's call this force your gremlin.

3

YOUR GREMLIN

Your gremlin is the source of the damn near incessant negative chatter in your head. Unlike your conscious mind, which you use to remember, rehearse, fantasize, and analyze, your gremlin is out to make you miserable by diverting you from enjoying the simple and glorious love vibrating within you during this and every moment of your life.

In 1984 I wrote a guidebook intended to help folks like you and me put this sleazy malcontent in his place. It is called *Taming Your Gremlin: A Guide to Enjoying Yourself.* The book you now hold is an elaboration on, and a continuation of, the process described in *Taming Your Gremlin.* The impetus for this writing is an outgrowth, in part, of letters and phone calls from people who have read *Taming Your Gremlin* and who have become conscious of their own undeniable, quite personal interaction with this wretch of the mind. For them, as it is for me *and for you,* consciously or unconsciously, gremlin taming is the ultimate undertaking, the pinnacle of challenges, the ultraconsequential campaign, the big kahoona, the top of the heap where adventure is concerned. Gremlin taming sits smack-dab in the middle of the mainstream of emotional as well as spiritual growth, and it is inherent in every activity, from climbing Mount

Everest to getting a good night's sleep. Gremlin taming is, in a phrase or three, the process of choosing light over darkness, good over evil, or, better yet, the love that sustains you over the fear that can destroy you. It's a meaty subject, to say the least, but one that is germane to your staying healthy and happy.

Your gremlin is probably, at this very moment, beginning to go wild. Your gremlin's sole purpose is to divert you from finding the simple love inside of you, and his (or her) job is a lot easier when he can hide outside of your awareness. He hates that I'm exposing him. Hear his chatter, but don't take it too seriously. He may say something like

"You already know what this guy has to say. Why read on? Close the book."

or

"You have more important things to do. Close the book."

or

"Life isn't a bowl of cherries. Settle for what you have. Close the book."

Well, he's wrong on all counts. Again, hear his chatter but don't take it too seriously. Simply notice it. Then make a choice to direct your awareness back to these words, back to your gremlin, or elsewhere. The key words here are *choice* and *awareness*. Your awareness is like a spotlight and you can place it wherever you like. The choice is yours. Learning to exercise gentle control over your awareness is an important skill when it comes to gremlin taming and to maximizing your enjoyment of your life. It is a skill you will sharpen throughout our time together and one that will help you observe your gremlin with a sense of detachment. If, at this moment, you're taking your gremlin too seriously and are having difficulty detaching from him, your breathing will be somewhat shallow and you will have a sense of blocked energy and/or tension in your shoulders, neck, head, chest, or stomach. Pay attention to it because—it's sad but true— tension handled improperly can threaten your life.

If you experience any of these symptoms or if you feel bored or frustrated, simply stop reading for a while. I'll be right here when you choose to saddle up for another ride. There's no hurry. Enjoying this life is a never-ending process at which you are going to get better and better. It's a process involving awareness and pleasure and love and absolutely cannot be forced. Trying, straining, working hard, gutting up, and figuring out are gremlin tools and are deterrents to finding the love and happiness you want. Allowing, noticing, letting up, and lightening up are aids in the gremlin-taming process.

Your gremlin will accompany you throughout this entire existence, so of course he will be with you and me throughout our time together. Remember, he doesn't want to learn from the advice that follows. But I have some news for you (and for him). Not only will you learn and benefit from what is ahead but, because your gremlin will be with you as you read on, you will be able to practice taming him on the spot.

Now that you have some sense of that bratlike gremlin of yours and, more importantly, of your ability to relegate him to the background of your experience when he rears his ugly head, I'd like to offer you some tips guaranteed to raise your level of contentment, reduce your stress, lessen your anxiety, liven up your relationships, increase your productivity, and free up your creativity.

4

CHOOSE TO BE HERE

Here you are, stumbling around on planet earth with the rest of us, carting your body along with you, playing all sorts of roles—such as mama, papa, teacher, therapist, up-person, down-person, lover, fighter, wild horse rider, and who knows what else—all the while immersed in the human condition, the condition that we here on earth seem to have some ironclad covert agreement never to discuss. If we did discuss it, however, the first line of the conversation might go something like this:

"I don't know about you, Bubba, but I'm lost."

Why you got shoved out onto this stage called life, an occupant of your particular body, in the midst of whatever unique drama you popped out into, I don't know. But you're here now, and while the props and players have probably changed somewhat since your arrival, your quests are essentially the same: to survive and to have a big time. To be a real champion of these endeavors, it will behoove you to first resolve a rather fundamental question: Do you want to be here? Shakespeare had Hamlet look this issue square in the eye when he had him call a spade a spade and say the words

"To be or not to be? That is the question."

Shakespeare had a way of weeding out the dead-wood. This "to be or not to be" question is a very important one and a very personal one, and while in our culture it's considered gloomy if not taboo to ponder it, doing so when you're feeling chipper can enliven your spirit. My guess is that you do want to be here and that that is precisely why you are here. Maybe you are here on earth to accomplish some important karmic task. Or then again, maybe you just stopped by for a cup of coffee. I don't know, and you may not know either. Or then again, maybe you knew but forgot. It would be no wonder. After all, you've been pretty busy since your arrival.

From the time you were pushed out sucking and gasping into this world, you've been the target of a constant (to put it mildly) barrage of experiences. From these experiences you've formed all sorts of ideas about who you are and who you should be and about how the world works and should work. Isn't it just possible that somewhere along the line the boundary between who you are and your *ideas* about who you are got blurred? Sure it is! But don't let it hang you up—at least you're here. Right here. Right now, ideas and all.

So, welcome. Welcome to this life and welcome to this moment. Would you like to stay on and leap off into the future? I hope so. But before deciding, you might first want to ask yourself something else: Can you have any fun here? Can you really enjoy this existence? Well, the answer is yes. Yes, you can. You'd better believe it. But it's tricky. This life is like the wind. Sometimes it blows like a bandit and often it changes direction suddenly. So, in order to feel secure and happy, you need to be well-grounded in something solid. You need to be grounded in an experience—an experience of who you really are. That is, the you that exists within your body but is not your body—the natural you.

13

5

THE NATURAL YOU

Your body will change. Mine has. (I used to weigh seven pounds, eight ounces.) And your personality will, too. And so will your preferences and your performance style, and the various roles you play. The real you is the one inside that miraculous mass of matter out of which you are now peering. The real me is inside my own body, which is at this moment holding a pen. From inside this sculpture of hair, eyes, teeth, gangly arms, and spindly legs, I'm choosing to write the words

"Hello in there."

You just pulled in through your eyes the words

"Hello in there."

The real you and the real me are, at this moment, smashing to smithereens the boundaries of time and space. Here I sit, on this day, in this house, communing with you; and there you be, on another day in another place in communion with me. The natural you understands the essence of my words. Your mind is busy making sense of them. Your gremlin, meanwhile, is gnashing his teeth and screeching something like "this is ridiculous." He's cranky and mean and he will do all in his power to bully or smooth-talk you off the path to purer pleasure. He would love to convince you to trust him instead of the natural you.

Your gremlin knows that, way back when you were a pretty unsophisticated, funny-looking rookie at this game of life, the natural you learned complex tasks like walking and talking, and did so without a smattering of knowledge about physics, kinesiology, or semantics. Your gremlin knows that the natural you is wise, pristinely pure, and sharp as a tack, and that the natural you holds the key to your happiness. To seduce you away from trusting the natural you, your gremlin will try to get you to dissect and analyze the meaning of these words. If you follow his lead you may get bored or confused. It's no big deal if this happens. Confusion is just your brain reacting to your gremlin's demand that you fit what you're reading into your brain's preconceived idea boxes about what you're reading. Your gremlin wants you to feel suspicious, parsimonious, piss-poor, and, ultimately, empty.

The natural you, on the other hand, is completely devoted to your survival and pleasure. The natural you is a pro at integrating wisdom and eliminating bunk. The natural you is nourished and guided by the true love within you. Its purpose is clear, even when your conscious mind is confused. The natural you recognizes the importance of simple enjoyment and that your enjoyment of your life is a do-it-yourself operation.

To increase your pleasure moment to moment and to start splashing around in that ocean of true love that is right inside of you right now, it will help to give enjoying yourself a top-notch, preferential spot on your list of priorities.

6

MAKE ENJOYING YOURSELF
A TOP PRIORITY

The more natural love you experience in any given moment the more you will enjoy yourself. Your gremlin will raise objections to this simple truth, and he may be doing so at this very moment. He wants you to feel lousy, so he may fuss, rant and rave, or hit you with some lengthy pseudointellectual pontification about how my message to you is overly simplistic. Notice his style. You may even gain some appreciation for his persistence and creativity. After all, he's been with you since your early years here in the Milky Way, and he's developed his methods based on his thorough knowledge of you and of your unique vulnerabilities. He is determined to hypnotize you into believing life is complex, difficult, and perhaps even painful, and he is a full-time devotee of his purpose. Notice his chatter, but do so without taking his chatter too seriously.

Your gremlin knows that if you get truly clear on your fundamental purpose—enjoying yourself—you are better than halfway home in the process of taming him. Self-enjoyment is a worthy but simple goal, and while it is not always easy to accomplish, it is not nearly so difficult as you might imagine once you see it as the motivating factor in every action you perform. You do what you do in an attempt to feel good. This is not only fine and dandy,

it is an essential truth, the awareness of which is fundamental to your happiness.

You probably carry with you a notion of what sort
of circumstances will fulfill you. Circumstances are configurations of the props and players in your life. Some circumstances you create, some you don't. Some you can
control, some you can't. Whether you are the sort who
likes to hobnob with the hoi-palloi, boogie with the good
ol' boys and girls, or knit, spit, or whittle all by yourself,
as you strive to form the props and players in your life into
circumstances that please you, it will be helpful to keep
in mind that doing so is a means to an end, not an end
in itself. You might strive for a hoity-toity mansion on a
tree-lined street, a cabin in the woods, a tiny waist, a
devoted lover, fame, naturally curly hair, or big biceps.
Fine. It's wise to have goals. Accomplishing them can
help you feel happy. But it's the happiness that you really
want—not the naturally curly hair or the big biceps. Your
longing for pleasure is why you developed the goals in
the first place.

"Of course," says that sleazy gremlin of yours. "You
know this stuff. Now let's you and me boogie."

Well, hang on. It's true you do know this already.
But you need reminding.

As you become more and more focused on your
number one priority—enjoying yourself—you will see
that making this goal depend only on certain circumstances means missing out on much of the pleasure available in every moment. *You can be happy now. You don't
have to wait.* And one of the first steps toward luxuriating
in the love and happiness that is inside you is to relax your
attachment to the pictures you carry around about how
life has to look in order for you to be content.

Your gremlin knows your favorite pictures and he's
right up there with Steven Spielberg and Woody Allen
when it comes to creating features suited to your taste. He
does so to keep you from enjoying the simple pleasure of

experiencing the real you in the real world, right here, right now.

While it is helpful to arrange the props and players in your life in a way that pleases you, when it comes to your sole purpose—enjoying your very own life—it comes in handy much more often to be skilled at maximizing your level of contentment regardless of the circumstances. To do so you must have a keen sense of where you end and the rest of the world (including your pictures about happiness) begins.

7

CLEARLY EXPERIENCE WHERE YOU END AND ALL ELSE BEGINS

On some level we are all one. Sounds like ethereal woo-woo, I know, but it's true. It doesn't mean you are me or I'm you. (I did try to be James Dean for a while in 1955, but my grin was too toothy.) It just means that we are all pure love, pure energy—pure love energy—and energy cannot be created (by earthlings, anyway) and cannot be destroyed. But—and this is an important *but*—on this physical plane of existence (the one where you go bowling and lose your keys), there is a miraculous sheath separating you from the rest of the world. It is a wonderful sheath. It is incredibly sensitive to the world that surrounds you. It is an amazing organ called—you guessed it—your skin.

Your skin has more nerve endings than any other part of your body. It is also waterproof and tough. Even when the top layer gets rubbed off, which it does constantly (you'll shed about forty disgusting pounds of dead skin in this lifetime), it is replaced by living layers below.

You exist within the boundary defined by this relatively thin organ. (It's about two millimeters thick in most places.) From inside your skin you are peering out at these words. In there you are breathing. In there you make choices. In there, at this moment, you will choose to read on or to stop. You would make this choice whether I mentioned it or not, and probably you would do so without consciously thinking about it. By mentioning it, however, I have brought it into your conscious mind and now you must make a conscious choice. Notice that it feels a little like work. Conscious choice has its benefits, but it requires energy. That's why requiring of yourself that you make too many choices can fry your circuits and manifest in symptoms such as alcoholism, ulcers, heart attacks, job burnout, car wrecks, and incoherent babbling. There is a difference in making a choice and in *trying* to make a choice, and perhaps you just experienced, in a subtle way, the difference. Perhaps you just learned or relearned the difference between effort and strain.

What is your experience at this moment? Are you relaxed and open so that the meaning of these words can float in through your eyes down to the natural you? Or are you ponderous and doubtful, restless, perhaps confused? Are you working hard to make meaning from these words? If the latter is true, your gremlin may be on the scene. If he's gotten to you, your breathing will be shallow and you may feel a sense of frustration. Either choose to focus on his chatter for a brief period of time or relax your breathing, focus on these words instead of his chatter, and read on.

In the next few days experiment with noticing your skin. Just be aware of it as a sensitive receptor and as a boundary within which you exist. The following exercise will help you do this. It will require your undivided attention, so after you read the instructions, put your book down, sit in a comfortable chair, and experiment.

21

Sit with your feet flat on the floor and your eyes closed. Your awareness is like a spotlight, and you have the ability to place it wherever you choose. Place your awareness on your breathing and begin following the path of your breath all the way in and all the way out of your lungs. Other stimuli such as sounds and your own thoughts will come into your awareness. If so, simply notice them, let them go, and place your awareness back on your breathing, making certain to take in all of the air you want and to exhale fully. To do so takes relaxed concentration. It requires effort but not strain. Allow your breathing to be the foreground of your experience and allow all else to fall into the background.

Once this is so, redirect your awareness to your fingertips and allow the sensations there to replace your breathing as the foreground of your experience. As you do so, allow your breathing to fade into the background. Notice how very sensitive your fingertips are. Keep your awareness on your fingertips for a breath or two until your fingertips become the most prominent objects of your awareness. Then, as you inhale, allow your awareness to expand to the palms of your hands, then to the tops of your hands, then to your forearms, and so on, until you become aware of your skin in its entirety. With practice, this process of becoming aware of the entire surface of your skin will require only the amount of time needed for one complete inhalation. As you complete the inhalation, shift your awareness to your eyelids and become aware of the weight of your eyelids on your eyeballs. Hold this awareness as you exhale fully. As you reach the end of this exhalation, very slowly lift your eyelids. Do so with an awareness of your skin as a very sensitive vibrating sheath between you and the world that surrounds you. You exist within the boundary defined by your skin, and from within that boundary you now have the opportunity to peer out and observe the world around you.

Experiment with bypassing your intellect and simply noticing the stimuli to which you are drawn. You may notice colors, shadows, sounds, smells, and textures. Shift your awareness slowly from one aspect of your environment to another. I've often referred to this process as "simply noticing." Simply noticing has nothing to do with analyzing and figuring out. Simply noticing means simply noticing. Consciously and gently shift your awareness and therefore the foreground of your experience from one aspect of your environment to another, and from time to time back to your breathing, making certain to take in all of the air that you want and to exhale fully. You may simply notice by using any of your senses—not just your eyes. Enjoy slowly shifting the foreground of your awareness from your visual field to the area around your ears. Drop your eyelids as you do so and allow sounds to drift in through your ears. As best you can, bypass your intellect. There is no need to think. Simply notice the sounds that drift in. You need not label them. Do the same with your senses of smell, taste, and touch.

Remain in touch with your skin as both a very sensitive receptor and as a boundary separating you from all else. This state of being has been called everything from "grounded" to "ginger-peachy." Let's you and I call it "being centered." It is simply one of the myriad states of being that are available to you and is not innately better or worse than others. It is, however, a wonderful tool for relieving anxiety and for creating within yourself a sense of healthy detachment from the world that surrounds you.

Centered, you can have a marvelous time slowly seeing, touching, smelling, hearing, and tasting selected aspects of the world. When centered, you can entertain yourself by doing something as simple as eating an orange, watching a sunset, or stroking the belly of someone who gets your motor humming. Have the experience *of* pure experience. Sink into the object of your attention using primarily one sense at a time. As you do so, gently shift your awareness back and forth from your breathing to your skin to the object, using each of your senses. Take your time and milk the experience for all it's worth. You'll like it.

Being centered can serve as a powerful home base to which you can return at will. It is a vantage point from which to view life. It may be helpful for you to think of the world as a three-dimensional movie into which you've just been plopped down. The world is filled with props and players, and you've entered the moment with your head filled with snapshots and notions that you can make as important as you want. You may participate in the movie to whatever degree you'd like. You may interact with the props and players in the movie to whatever extent you choose, and you can create your own style of doing so.

Now that you have a clearer sense of where you end and all else begins, let's cast our focus on the world that surrounds you.

8

OBSERVE YOUR PROPS
AND PLAYERS

Think of the world as filled with props and players. There are millions of props and players in your world. They interrelate with one another and with you to form circumstances. Many of these circumstances affect your challenge of having *beaucoups* of love and joy in your life.

There are those times when you stride with pride, basking in the glory of having (or at least imagining you have) your proverbial ducks in a neat, dutiful row. But let one of those little quackers go waddling off in a direction discordant with your scheme, and you'll begin to fret. If you're the go-get-'em sort, you may even be moved to action and shoo the rebel duck back under your wise leadership. If two or three ducks charge off, get lost, croak, or hatch their own babies, however, your anxiety level is sure to shoot sky high and you will fret about how in the dickens you can get these little palookas to realize you're the boss and to straighten up and fly right. Sometimes you can. Other times you simply can't. Really. You can't. Not if your sense of a straight line is different from what the universe has in mind, and God only knows what the universe has in mind. The hard truth is, the tidbits of substance and life you can control are few and far between, and it's pretty silly, given the magnitude and mystery of the universe, for you and I to stomp around down

here pounding our chests and acting like we're in total command. Now, don't misunderstand me. You have some definite choices as to where to place your props and players and about how to respond to circumstances. And you have responsibility for your choices. But when it comes to your number one priority—enjoying yourself—it is more helpful than I can say to differentiate from moment to moment and from situation to situation what you can control and what you can't.

I recall a crisp, sunny Saturday morning not long ago, a day in which feeling the love within was coming easy. I meditated, ran, had a fine breakfast with my wife and son, and got myself ready to drive from my home near Dallas to Austin, Texas, to conduct a workshop. I felt content, free, clear, loving, and wise. Life was a bowl of cherries. There I was, gliding down the highway listening to the Supremes, when I was abruptly and rudely assaulted by a blaring horn.

Even if you've but a rudimentary knowledge of highway etiquette, you are no doubt aware of a honk continuum bounded on the one end by a polite "I hate to interrupt, but we really must move along now" beep and on the other end by a "move it or lose it" blast that lasts. The tone of this blaring intrusion placed it solidly into the latter category. My neck muscles grew tight as baseball twine—a reflex action, an attempt to pull my head inside my body. My knuckles turned white as my grip on the wheel intensified. My eyes were wide. My skin was tight. Then I saw him. He sped by on my left, guffawed, shot me the bird, and leaned on his horn before cutting back in front of me and goosing it. He seemed to be having a big time at my expense.

He was driving a small truck with huge wheels. (I have a wild man's disdain for this type of vehicle. They remind me of cockroaches, and I think they should be squashed.) The driver was young, skinny, and ugly. His rear window brandished a gun rack and a rebel flag decal, and while I only got a glance at his teeth, I'm sure they were crooked and stained. I did not love this human. I had been in my own lane, traveling the speed limit, innocent, thinking pure and noble thoughts and minding my own business. In an instant, the blissful feeling I had relished all morning was kicked aside in favor of momentary fear, and the fear hardly settled in before it was sent tumbling by a passionate urge to maim.

Not only had my life flashed before my eyes, but now my gremlin had me totally convinced that my manhood was on the line. Miraculous how it had happened. In three or maybe four seconds, I had been transformed from a mild-mannered, love-filled, benevolent Saint Francis kind of guy into an angry pit bull. I wanted to squash that mini-truck and chew off the face of its pea-brained driver. I wanted to make him beg. I wanted revenge, dammit. My gremlin squealed "Punch his lights out," and once again the queen bee of misery-making myths had a death grip on my psyche. Ah, I know her well: The old "I'll feel at peace again when, and only when, I straighten him/her/they/it (depending on the circumstances) out."

I've experienced many variations on the theme, but usually it boils down to the belief that my peace of mind depends on my being publicly proclaimed as "right," although I've also been known to hold out for being uncompromisingly pronounced "most righteous" and, in earlier days, "cool." It's a paradoxical stance at best, since it results in my surrendering without a fight, to the props and players in my world, total power over where I will be placed on the pain/pleasure yardstick of existence.

It's true that, like it or not, circumstances affect my moment-to-moment level of contentment—and yours, too, I'll bet. To be sure, I for one am a devotee of the "if you don't like your circumstances, change them" point of view. But where enjoying this life is concerned, I'm into expediency. I'm an addict hooked on peace of mind, and an addict will stop at nothing. So maybe, just maybe, I could feel good even if this scum-suckin' truck-driving

28

low-life sped off into the future without seeing that, on this trail, on this day, I was wearing the white hat and he was a slithering snake in the grass.

To feel good when your ego has been tweaked isn't easy. It takes, above all else, sincere intention. On that fateful Saturday I pulled it off. (Which makes for a dull ending to this tale, I know, but we're here to learn, not just be entertained, right?) I let the dirtball truck driver drift to the background of my experience, took a deep breath, and settled back into a relative state of calm contentment. Remembering my number one priority helped. Centering myself helped. The Supremes helped. It was a small victory, I know—a practice run and one hardly comparable to illness, divorce, death of a loved one, war, or famine; but the game is the same and the point is a simple one: While it is admirable to attempt to arrange your props and players according to your preferences, when it comes to your number one priority, enjoying your life, it is even more admirable to be able to regulate your level of contentment even if your circumstances aren't cooperating.

The key is to become adept at controlling the attitudes and actions of the one player you *can* control—you. It's a challenge, but one with a rapidly ascending learning curve—if you practice.

Life is a river on a rampage, so I'd be the last one to suggest that yours is about to become a fun-filled stream of zany capers. It's not. Or that you will always feel jolly. You won't. But in any situation, regardless of how shocking or difficult, you can maximize your sense of well-being and minimize your displeasure if you will make conscious your number one priority—to enjoy yourself—as well as attend to where you end and all else begins, simply notice your gremlin, observe your props and players, and breathe, dammit, breathe!

9

BREATHE,
DAMMIT, BREATHE!

Eventually you will stop breathing and your body will rot. Until then, make certain to take in all of the fresh air your body needs and desires, and to exhale fully. How and what you breathe affects your health and your disposition. Proper breathing for healthy people under healthful circumstances comes easy. Millions of happy infants and sound-sleeping grown-ups do it constantly without effort. As for you, if you take into your lungs too little good, clear oxygen, you are sure to get tense, blue, and probably ill. If you take in too much without expelling it completely, you will get woozy and act strange.

When you take into your system plenty of fresh air and oxygen, you send the oxygen, via your lungs, to your veins and arteries. You are doing so right now. The blood going from your lungs through your arteries at this moment is just as red as can be, because it is about one-fourth oxygen. In the few seconds since you began reading this chapter, your heart has pushed streams of blood (and oxygen) through your arteries and capillaries to the cells making up your body.

Here in brief is some of what goes on in a healthy body, and why I'm making such a big deal out of you taking the time to attend to your breathing. The oxygen within the rich, red blood in your arteries is traded to the cells in all parts of your body for waste material. The waste-laden blood becomes a dull blue and travels back to the right side of your ticker, which pumps it into the blood vessels in your lungs. When the blood encounters more oxygen, it releases the toxic carbon dioxide and takes in the oxygen. The freshly purified blood is then returned to the left side of your heart and once again is pumped out to all parts of your body.

My first draft of this chapter contained an elaborate breathing exercise, but I chucked it. Its explanation took too many words and breathing is such a fundamental (and important) experience that writing *about* it felt like trying to French kiss over the telephone. Here's what I'd like you to know.

Full, clear breathing is important. It entails liberal and lively movement of your abdomen, outwardly as you inhale and inwardly as you exhale. This sounds backward to some people and it may to you. Your tendency may be to pull your abdomen in when you inhale and force it out when you exhale. This stomach-in, chest-out style of inhalation allows you to fill only the upper portions of your lungs. It is a breathing style that is common to all of us when we feel threatened, but folks who breathe this way habitually are often people who are perpetually fearful and suspicious—usually because of hurtful past experiences. They tend to distrust themselves and others. This type of breathing and the bodily tension that accompanies it are an attempt to brace against life rather than to live in it.

Thinking and feeling are both noble activities, and a balance between both is essential for your fulfillment, pleasure, and productivity. When you cramp your breathing you block feeling and limit your ability to sense and fully experience the world around you. Your awareness becomes concentrated in your intellect rather than in your body and sensory receptors. We all do this to some extent at times, such as when we are grappling with some unresolved issue from our past, analyzing a di-

lemma, or trying too hard to predict and mentally prepare for the future. These cerebral processes are important and have their place in controlled doses, but too much analysis, fantasy, or past or future thought can result in your missing this life as it is unfolding for you right here and right now, and can make you anxious and fretful. Too much time in thought can result in your spending an unhealthy portion of your life in your head instead of in the world. While your conscious mind is a humdinger of a gift, it's important to remind yourself that *it* belongs to *you.* You're not your brain, though I hasten to add that you would be a bore without it. Proper breathing can help you maintain an efficient balance between your use of your intellect and your use of your natural senses.

Your awareness of your breathing is a remarkably efficient method for monitoring how well you are doing the job of remaining cool, calm, collected, and content, and for increasing your overall level of pleasure in any given moment. It's worth attending to. No doubt about it, when your breathing is relaxed and clear and you are taking in all of the air you want and exhaling fully (without hyperventilating), you will be more aware of yourself, more aware of the props and players in your world, more aware of where you end and they begin, and, most importantly, more open to the love within and the love-stimulating experiences available in the world.

If clear, full, relaxed breathing has not been your habit, you may find when you try it that you feel uncomfortably vulnerable. In the Western hemisphere especially, we are socialized into tensing in anticipation of pain, as if this will prevent or lessen the pain we fear. Bogus information. To tense against pain is counterproductive. Tensing, in fact, initiates, perpetuates, and prolongs pain. Experiment with thinking of the experience you may have heretofore labeled as "vulnerable" as a simple state of relaxed attentiveness or, in the words of Fritz Perls, "creative indifference." The part of me that wants to appear high, spiritual, and hip would like to add that pain is only pain. The part of me who is middle-aged, married, and lives in the suburbs, however, feels compelled to add that pain—for all its growth-producing side effects—hurts like hell, and I'd rather lead my life without it. I can't. But I've learned, as have many of my clients, friends, and others, that it's possible to weaken its wallop by relaxing your body, clearing your breathing, and giving the pain room to do its thing.

Your breathing can serve you as both a barometer and a regulator of the extent to which you dive into an all-out experience of your life. Notice differences in your breathing as you encounter one situation after another—like during lovemaking or in a negotiation with someone you distrust. Experimenting with proper breathing, while simple, can be invigorating and, in a way, confronting. It can, in fact, become a wrestling match between you and that archenemy of yours, your gremlin. Your gremlin has no patience for this sort of experimentation, since he knows that, by attending to your breathing, you can send him scurrying and take a giant step in the direction of pleasure and away from anguish. He may push you to hurry through this chapter or even to stop reading. He may come charging in with combat boots, hollering at you to jump and fight some more windmills. If so, simply choose to direct your awareness back to my words, to your breathing, or choose to go ahead and listen to your gremlin, or even to accommodate his wishes. You might actually find his chatter entertaining or gain some appreciation for his creativity and persistence. But, for goodness' sake, don't waste time haggling with your gremlin, now or ever. That's what he wants you to do, and if he can berate, challenge, or seduce you into doing combat with him you can spend precious moments of your life engulfed in a state of disgruntled confusion instead of in a state of relaxed pleasure. Simply choose to do what your gremlin wants or what you want.

Choose is the key word here. Make a conscious choice. If you are not enthusiastic about reading further or experimenting with focusing on your breathing, don't. You can read more when you're next in the mood. While your stay in the galaxy is temporary, throughout it you will be breathing, so you can choose to focus on your breathing at any time.

When you do choose to experiment with your breathing, get into it. Practice. It's important. You can read this book or others until you're a walking, talking, enviable encyclopedia of facts and philosophies on the betterment of humankind, and while you might impress your friends with your library and your vocabulary, none of the knowledge you gather will amount to a hill of beans unless you get serious enough to turn theory into action through practice. The word is not the thing, nor the description the described, when it comes to enjoying your life. So wait until you are ready to experiment and then give it a "champeen" effort.

Relaxed breathing coupled with an awareness of your skin as both a boundary and a receptor will help you feel calm, alert, aware, and present—in short, centered. In fact, these simple awarenesses are so powerful that with practice you can learn to greatly reduce the physical manifestations of fear and anxiety by simply attending to them.

Even if you are feeling centered, your breathing is clear, and you are acutely aware of where you end and all else begins, unpredictable shifts of props, players, and circumstances can feel like a threat, shove you off center, and throw you into an anxious fit or a low-down funk. Whether your moments of misery are brought about by your own mind games or some sort of real-world frenzy, with practice you can become masterful at recentering. It requires effort—more under some circumstances than others—but you can have a good time practicing. Start under easy circumstances and work up to tougher ones. Practice in a variety of settings.

When you are ready to experiment, take a few moments to center yourself and to clear your breathing.

Then, as you move through your daily activities, coming into contact with various players in your world, notice changes in your breathing. Experiment with staying centered and, when necessary, with restoring a feeling of centeredness in a variety of circumstances by simply attending to and regulating your breathing and by attending to your skin as both a sensitive receptor and a boundary. You might, for example, notice your breathing while in a conversation with a trusted friend; in an encounter with someone you perceive as having some control over your livelihood, such as an employer; or, best of all, in an argument with anybody. Interpersonal conflicts are dynamite opportunities for practicing keeping your breathing clear and staying centered. While such conflicts on occasion carry the genuine threat of physical harm, in our relatively civilized society what is more likely to be on the line is your ego. In such circumstances I like to remember the wise words of an inspiring writer, artist, and musician named Terry Allen, who said, "My ego ain't my amigo."

We all have our ideas about who we are and who we're supposed to be. Our self-concept changes from time to time, but when its existence is threatened, our tendency is to fight with frantic fervor to preserve it. When the self-image you cling to is threatened, your breathing is sure to get cramped and shallow. This is both a symptom and a cause of tension. It can tell you that you are imagining that your well-being is on the line, and it can be an aid in helping you recenter.

Recentering under these circumstances can help you avoid getting your act—your "advertising"—confused with your God-given life. The distinction between your life and your act is an important one, and unless you remain conscious of it in the midst of dissonant circumstances, you will scrape to preserve your act with the same ardor with which you would fight to save your life. This bit of universal insanity is as common as navel lint, and I see it played out time and time again in my work with couples, families, and organizations.

As for my own experience, I have chunks of memory cells weighed down by more painful examples of this quirk than I care to recall, but in the next chapter is one I'll hazard in the service of honesty, your pleasure, and our mutual quest for a better hereafter.

10

IF YOU CAN'T RUN WITH THE BIG DOGS, KEEP YOUR ASS ON THE PORCH

I grew up in what was then a small west Texas town. While those were the olden days before Pac Man and rampant teenage fornication, like today's red-blooded youth we were sex-crazed and strange. I was, anyway. I would have crawled a hundred yards over broken glass to flick a pretty girl's tongue with my own, and it was clear to me then that to do so I'd first have to win her favor. Back then, to my mind, anyway, the prevailing mentality in which a sixteen-year-old boy set out to define his identity and prove his prowess was summed up by the phrase "If you can't run with the big dogs, keep your ass on (or better yet, under) the porch."

The big dogs in my high school had flattops, low foreheads, big necks, and were varsity football players. I had wavy hair, a high forehead, a big neck, and made the varsity football team by the skin of my teeth. Only my neck didn't get big from something run of the mill like farmwork or inbreeding. My neck got that way because I ordered a neck strap and barbells from Joe Weider Products and worked out like a madman in an attempt to flee from my endomorphic natural state into the ranks of the big dogs so that, like them, I could strut through the

halls with an adoring frosty-haired pom-pom girl on my arm or, better yet, fate willing, hold her warm and tender body next to mine.

We all know about reaching the first three bases and home, but the latter was nearly off-limits to my way of thinking in 1959. In 1959 even the term *sexual intercourse* drew gasps and snickers, and while on occasion my dates and I turned the term into a living experience, more often we would get close to doing so and freeze like ice sculptures. I might get VD, she might get PG, and even worse yet — found out — neither of us would get elected to the student council and then we'd never get to be "pop-lar." So most of the time we skipped home base and started around the bases again. On occasion the universe showered me with favor, and I got to wallow in the pleasure of a prolonged, wild, and rampant mutual backseat leg hump, seasoned with moans, groans, squirms, and wet-talk. It usually crescendoed in a flurry of clothes-rumpling activity and quick zips until, at short last, the raging river merged with the calm sea and the whole event was hidden under my untucked shirttail, never to be mentioned by her or me.

I don't want to imply that I was no more than an uncouth hunk of carnal impulse—but I was. At least I was much of the time. My gentler side was around somewhere, even then—I just didn't know how to fit it in with my big dog disguise, and it didn't take much stimulation from fact or fantasy to get me so torqued-up with testosterone that brain power and better judgment took a way-backseat to an all-consuming intrigue with the fairer sex.

By my junior year, I had developed a fair to middlin' big dog disguise and had become a mildly sought after and somewhat prideful pooch. I was a happy pup. Happy indeed . . . until, at the end of our first date, I kissed Sally, then looked into her eyes. I got lost in them and felt weak-kneed, shaky, dazed, hot, mellow, and permeated with love and lust. I fell head over heels for Sally. She became the focus of my existence. I lived to watch her walk, touch her, kiss her, smell her, and put my lively tongue in her dainty little ear. Then after our third date I experienced a new set of feelings. I started to *like* her. Really like her. I even liked her wit and the wisdom with which she spoke. I'd liked girls before, but this much like and lust all at once shook me up. I liked everything about Sally, a response for which I was totally unprepared. It threw me. I knew well enough how to hump a girl's leg, but I hadn't the foggiest notion what to do with a whole girl—so mostly I just flexed my neck and floated on fantasies of Sally.

Sally consumed my every thought for about six months. I consumed her every thought for about six weeks. I remember the day Sally's feelings seemed to shift.

Sally was on her front porch and I was about ten feet away on a walkway which led from her porch to the curb where my fuchsia-and-white 1955 Ford was parked. It was lowered in front, pinstriped, and had a spider painted on the dashboard. It must have been a warm day because Sally was wearing shorts and I remember ogling her lovely, oh-so-strokable, creamy, smooth, voluptuous, just-right thighs, the thought of which made me even warmer.

There I stood, drinking in Sally with my eyes, testosterone running rampant. I tried to look cool as a cucumber, while flexing my neck. I flexed it hard. It wasn't a first-class coil of muscle, but it wasn't small, either. (Though it may have looked small compared to my biceps. I could make my left bicep look like a Christmas ham by propping it up on the window ledge of my Ford. I know because I used to drive past store windows to check it out.) I stood facing Sally with my thumbs hung in the front pockets of my Levi's and my shoulders humped forward in an attempt to give maximum expansion to my neck and look happy-go-lucky at the same time. My feet were parallel and placed a little wider than shoulder width apart. Great stance. Great act. Then, whammo! From out of nowhere she zapped me. A straight shot to my bravura. Sally looked at me puzzled-like and asked, "Why are you standing like that?"

My breathing stopped. How'd she know I was standing "like that"? Was I that transparent? I thought I looked loose as a goose, muscular, cool, and kind of tough. Could she tell I was faking it? Could she tell I was flexing my neck to the point of impending paralysis?

There I stood, caught like a rat in a trap. I held my bluff. What could I say, "Oh, I'm just flexing my neck and trying to look like a big dog so you'll let me hump your leg again soon"? Absolutely not. I maintained my pose. Full flex. My armpits started dripping, and I could feel my neck muscles cramping up.

"Like what?" I mumbled, bobbing my head up and down, faking a what-kind-of-stupid-question-is-that look.

"Like that, Rick. You're standing funny. You look tense or something," she said.

I tried to look unaffected, nonchalant, and sort of intensely sullen—like Marlon Brando in *On The Waterfront.* I continued to bob my head around, all the while looking to the side, then up toward the sky, then back to her. A ploy. My feeble attempt to poo-poo her half-baked notion that I was anything less than naturally natural. Then our eyes met. The moment of truth. She wasn't fooled. Panicked and embarrassed, I froze. My gonads skittered upward, seeking shelter. My big dog act was on the line. My manhood was on the chopping block and the axe was in Sally's hand. It was fight, flight, or fess-up time. The latter was out of the question. I sighed, threw my head back, and sort of rolled my eyes. It worked for Brando, it could work for me.

"I gotta split," I said.

Then I turned and headed slowly for my car. It seemed like a very long walk. Walking and trying to look relaxed while flexing one's neck with all one's might takes finesse. Opening a car door, getting in, starting the car, and driving away while staying flexed takes Buddhist concentration.

Things were never the same with Sally and me after that. She had seen right through me—probably not for the first time, but it was the first time I had seen her see right through me. I couldn't stand it. What if she saw that I was just a clumsy, scared sixteen-year-old kid wrapped in a muscled-up suit of armor with big biceps and a tense neck? What if she saw that I wasn't a big dog at all? So what did I do? From then on I flexed harder every time I was with Sally. Not just with my neck—but with my whole psyche. Before a comment left my lips I sanded it smooth of any sign of gentleness. I think I was even rude most of the time. And remember, I liked her, I really liked her. It became no fun for me or for her. I flexed so hard that the love and the like in my heart got cramped. It couldn't get out. Before long I just faded right out of Sally's life and she out of mine. It's hard to have much fun when you're flexing all the time.

11

RELAX YOUR PACT TO KEEP YOUR ACT INTACT

I've met big dogs, beauties, bad girls, lovable lugs, sensitive males, new women, beboppers, yups, hunks, metaphysical magi, earth mothers, effervescent evangelists, and more. We've all got our acts and they change from time to time; but, lordy, don't take your act too seriously or, when it gets blasted by folks or fits of fate, you'll get defensive and probably make an ass out of yourself, all in the service of keeping your act intact.

John Prine had a good point when he sang, "You are what you are and you ain't what you ain't." A pithier statement on the same theme was engraved at the Delphic oracle as "Know Thyself." We've all got our advertising, our facade, the numbers we run. They're part of humanhood. But you'll feel better and have far more enjoyable relationships if you'll allow the natural you lots of space to come out and roam about. Let your act reflect you, your preferences, and your ideas rather than some trumped-up version of how you imagine you're supposed to be. As for me, I'm happy my encounter with Sally happened at least at a relatively early stage in my life. It taught me an important lesson about authenticity.

What if I had told Sally what I felt? What if I had said, "I think you're beautiful and smart as a whip and I like you. I really like you."

Would she have squealed and run away screaming? Would she have called me a wimp? Would she have nibbled my lower lip? Who knows? I don't. You don't either, and Sally probably couldn't even tell us. Even if I'd come through with the poignant poetry of a Cyrano, the relationship may have soured. After all, I'd been flexing in lots of ways throughout my relationship with Sally. Encounters like these are unpredictable. That's probably why expressing to someone your thoughts and feelings about them has been called "taking a risk." It's not like kayaking down the Green River, but still, when you express what is true for you about another person, you don't know if you're going to get roses or rotten tomatoes, especially if what you're revealing is more confrontational than complimentary. So why do it? It's exciting, that's why, and the possibilities that it opens up can knock your socks off. It gives others the opportunity to know and like you rather than just to applaud or reject your act, and it gives you at least a shot at intimacy. It opens up the possibility of love, and often it feels terrific—like coming out of a dark hiding place, a place where you're safe but bored. It's a way of popping out of your disguise (pleasant though your disguise may be), landing on your feet in front of another breathing, feeling human being, and saying, "I'm me and I'm here. Who and where are you?" It gives others a chance to know you and it invites them to come out and cavort with you. Over the last several years, one client after another has bombarded me with reams of reasons why this sort of open display of selfhood is dangerous, if not downright foolhardy. And maybe sometimes it is. I'll admit it. But most of the objections I've heard don't hold water.

One client of mine finally got my drift and made an admirable, gutsy, perhaps even overzealous run at unabashedly putting himself "out there" by giving a woman he adored, but had dated for only two months, a full-length mink coat. While this gentleman is well-heeled, he is not rolling in dough, nor is he weak-minded. But he is loving and knows himself well enough to know that he derives great pleasure from giving. He described to me in detail how much he enjoyed planning the purchase, picking the coat out, and picturing it on the lovely lady of his dreams. When he surprised her with the coat, she stammered and stuttered and said she didn't know if she should keep it. He just kept looking at her, beaming with glee at the pleasure of giving it to her and the excitement inherent in the unpredictability of the moment, until it occurred to him that she wanted him to resolve her discomfort by insisting that she keep the coat or return it to him. But this man is a clear thinker. He knows where he ends and others begin. He just kept smiling and said something like, "Oh, that's up to you. That's your part. My part was to give it to you."

She loved the coat (and as it turned out, him as well). In the process they both learned something about responsibility, which is really no more than "response-ability." You can greatly enhance your "response-ability" and the clarity and simplicity of your life by at least strongly considering giving honest expression to your feelings and letting others select and take responsibility for their responses to you. To not consider potential consequences for your actions would, of course, be less than wise. But remember, catastrophic expectations, like dreams of glory, all occur in a fantastic field of make-believe. If you imagine the field is filled with land mines, you are likely to freeze in one spot and forget that while life, sure enough, is one damn thing after another, it does not have to be the same damn thing over and over again.

I'm not big on rules, especially rules for something as ever-evolving as life on planet earth, and I would be the last one to tell you to always be open or to always be closed when you're wondering whether to act on your thoughts and feelings about others. The key, once again, is that you have a choice. But before choosing to play it safe time after time by keeping your feelings and opinions to yourself, or being oh-so-cautious in how you express them, at least consider the potential for pleasure and excitement you might get from the simple act of wide-open expression—with words or actions.

Simple, honest, open expression can be both risky and growth producing—especially in the context of a conflict with someone you value.

12

RESOLVE CONFLICT: OBSERVE YOUR FEELINGS

Conflict is as natural as nighttime, but unresolved conflict can lead to folks being disgruntled, bummed out, anxious, angry, and frustrated. Left to seethe beneath the surface, these feelings can and do rain havoc on family relationships and friendships. In the workplace, conflict ignored or handled improperly leads to self-serving attitudes, grumbling, tardiness, wasted time, poor job performance, unproductive cliques, scapegoating, unnecessary sick leave, and employee turnover—in other words, poor morale. And poor morale is very expensive. It's a weighty subject, this conflict thing, but one that is pertinent to your quest for pleasure, so let's get after it.

Read the instructions that follow and then close your eyes and do as they suggest. If that gremlin of yours whines "I don't wanna" or drones something like "How passé, I've done this sort of thing," dust him off with an "Oh, dry up" glare and then direct your attention back here.

Simply focus on your breathing for a few breaths, following the path of your breath all the way into your system and all the way out, making certain to exhale fully. Use some relaxed concentration to keep your awareness on your breathing for a few breaths. As thoughts come into your awareness, just let them go. After following a few breaths into your system and out again, shift your spotlight of awareness from your breathing to your fingertips and then allow them to occupy the foreground of your experience for a breath or two. Then expand your awareness until you experience your skin in its entirety. At that point, move your awareness from your skin into your imagination.

Bring into your imagination an image of someone with whom you are currently in conflict—be the conflict a full-blown battle or a nit-picking tiff. The object of your snit may be someone you hardly know or someone you know very well. It may even be someone you love wholeheartedly, but whom you are not liking very much right now. Take a good look at the image you conjure up of this person. Really notice him or her. This person can't see you, so really take the opportunity to look. Notice this person's face and pay special attention to the eyes and to the area around the eyes. Notice what you feel as you look at this person. Go slow. Be aware of what you want to do as you encounter this person—of your tendency. Pay special attention to any changes in your breathing as you view this person's image and to what you feel around your heart and in the pit of your stomach.

Having done this, open your eyes, get some paper and a pen or pencil, and jot down your reactions. Do this before reading further.

Now read the following instructions and then re-enter your fantasy, again picturing the person with whom you are in conflict.

In your mind's eye, tell the other person precisely what you are thinking and feeling about him or her. Be completely honest. You need not worry about being fair, gentle, right, or righteous. This is not a rehearsal for life. It's not a role play. It is a fantasy. Let yourself have the experience of authentic expression. Be honest with yourself and honest with the other person. Notice the effect on your breathing and on the rest of your body as you open up and fully express yourself. Have the experience of authenticity rather than the experience of attempting to derive a particular response from the other party. Continue until you have expressed yourself completely, and then—once again—write some notes from your experience. Take your time and see what emerges for you.

Read the next instructions and then, once again, close your eyes and re-enter the fantasy.

Picture the person with whom you are in conflict and imagine a full-blown, genuine response from him or her, a response in which the person shoots straight with you, sharing his or her reaction not only to what you said but to you as a person. Even if in reality the other person tends to be an inexpressive sort, imagine that for the moment the person's mask is off and he or she is being completely honest, unguarded, and uncensored—unprotective of his or her ego, or of yours. Notice this person's facial expression and voice, and notice what happens in your body as you do so. Be willing to fully experience the person and his or her impact on you. Notice the effect on your body and especially on your breathing. Take your time with this experience and then open your eyes and jot down some notes regarding the contact and the impact of this person's verbal and nonverbal message to you. In doing your writing, use words and phrases that have meaning to you, remembering that they needn't make sense to anyone else. This learning experience is a personal one, just for you.

What did the object of your discontent have to say about you? How does it feel to consider these things? Does what was said fit for you? Be honest with yourself. Did the other person point out a quality or three of yours that you have a difficult time accepting? If so, is it a quality or tendency that you would like to modify? Beginning when?

Read the following and then go back into the fantasy again.

Picture the other person and begin expressing your feelings about this person directly to him or her. Do so fully and completely, but do so this time without words. Let your body be totally expressive, yet nonverbal. If you circumvented your intellect and simply allowed your body to do its thing without words, what would it do? Would you shake the other person, pulverize him or her, plant a big kiss on his or her cheek, kick his or her shins? Be honest with yourself. Whatever you imagine doing is fine. There is no way to do this activity wrong. This is just a fantasy. *Your* fantasy. Give yourself permission to dive into it and to learn from it. Open your eyes now and jot down your observations. Be reflective and honest and, again, take your time.

To get closure on this experience, read the next instructions and experiment with doing as they suggest.

Picture the person with whom you are in conflict standing about fifteen feet away from you. See this person, feeling centered and secure. Have a sense of detachment from this person. Look into his or her eyes and get a feeling for this person as a life inside a body. Be aware of where you end and of the space between you and the person. Imagine a beam of white light emanating from behind your heart, upward into your head, out through your eyes. Imagine a similar beam of light passing from behind the other person's heart, up to his or her head, out through the eyes. See the beams meeting somewhere between the two of you and see the beams merge perfectly together. Allow yourself to sense the "natural one" within the other person's body. See this person as an independent traveler like yourself, as a pure soul who, like you, is encased in a body and who views life through a veil of concepts about him- or herself and the world—a soul with whom you have crossed paths. You needn't ponder the experience, simply glimpse it and then allow the image to fade. As it fades, gently but purposefully direct your awareness back to your breathing, taking in all of the air you want and exhaling fully. Do this for two or three complete breaths and then shift your awareness to your eyelids. Notice the weight of your eyelids on your eyeballs. Expand your awareness to the skin covering your entire body. Attend to your skin as a sensitive receptor. Feel the air on your skin and clothes on your skin. Now attend to your skin as a boundary—a sheath separating you from all else. Become aware of your presence back in the here and now, and when you are ready, lift your eyelids.

I suggest that you now jot down some further notes about your experience. Take the time to reflect on the questions that follow and write down your responses.

> From your experience in these fantasies, what generalizations can you draw about how you tend to handle conflict?
>
> What are your fears where uncensored, open expression is concerned?
>
> How was it for you to give full rein to your feelings?
>
> What did you feel like at the point you were about to hear what the other person thought about you?
>
> What did he or she have to say about you?
>
> When you censor yourself, what are your considerations?
>
> On what experiences are those considerations based?
>
> What are your catastrophic expectations regarding conflict?
>
> What are your fears (if any) regarding the expression of anger?
>
> How was conflict handled between your parents?
>
> How was conflict handled between your parents and you?
>
> How was conflict handled between you and your siblings?
>
> When you are in conflict with someone, how old do you feel?
>
> How big or little?

I suggest you do some stream-of-consciousness writing about your experience of yourself in conflict. See what thoughts, feelings, and images emerge. Be open to discovery.

The experience of conflict brings forth a range of emotions, not the least of which is anger. Anger is energy, and given the space to do its thing within you, it can empower and enliven you. If you habitually legislate against it within yourself, it can make you disgruntled, nervous, or ill. If you express it without consideration for others and their property you may get your lovin' self into trouble or find yourself alone more often than you like. Tune in to yourself enough to experience your anger and to feel it fully. Breathe and let it run rampant through your body. Give it lots of space within you. Remember that anger is energy and that you have an infinite number of choices about what to do with it. Among the simpler ones are expressing it verbally and congruently (allowing your voice and facial expression to match the feelings), and simply experiencing it and enjoying the surge of energy without tensing up and giving yourself a pain in the neck or head, an attack of colitis, an ulcer, a heart attack, or some other physical malady. Anger can be an incredible thing to behold, not just in yourself, but in others. It reddens faces, raises voices, and sometimes clears the air. How folks close to you handle it affects the quality of their lives and yours.

Al Carson was a near master of contentment—its creation, its preservation, and when need be, its rapid restoration. When I was a little boy, he was huge and powerful in my eyes, a distant figure with flashing eyes and a dancing smile. He wore suit coats that were warm to the touch, and he smoked Max Seller cigars. Al Carson was my dad. We lived in the same house but in different worlds.

As I grew taller, Al grew shorter and balder, and more wrinkled, but his disposition stayed as light, vibrant, and clear as the sparkle in his eyes. His anger rarely surfaced, but when it did, he was transformed—like Clark Kent into Superman, only quicker, because he didn't have to change clothes first. It happened suddenly, in the blink of an eye, and lasted only a few seconds—like a switch had been tripped. His upper lip twitched, his teeth flashed bright white, and light shot out of his eyes. He grew taller and broader on the spot. He looked lethal and cocksure, and he moved like lightning. It was beautiful. It made me quake with fear and shiver with delight all at once, even when I was the object of the fire in his soul. It only happened once or twice a year, but it was worth the wait.

Al only touched me twice in anger. He slapped my face both times. I'm not big on hitting and feel that causing others pain is pretty much an across-the-board bad idea, but in both of these instances I had it coming. In fact, I should have been drawn and quartered, but that wasn't Al's way. He figured my life was mine and his was his, so he got miffed only if I interfered with him, and stayed angry only until the interference was cleared up. That sort of efficiency in intention and action is rare. It lends clarity and simplicity to life. It is both the basis and symbol of what we call confidence and was, I think, the magic key to Al's almost perpetual contentment. And to the happiness that pervaded our family life.

As you continue to stroll and occasionally stumble through life, pay attention to the emotions you experience in conflictive situations and to your habitual responses to those emotions. Then, if you choose to do so—change, for a change. Play with options. Fool around. Become aware of any fear you have of being fully true to yourself. Attend to it as it plays through your mind and body and, for goodness' sake, don't tell yourself you must change. Just experience your anger and your fears regarding its expression. Notice your fears with a sense of detachment. Consider their validity based on the current situation. Then—for kicks—once in a while, change just for a change. If, for instance, your habit has been to scare yourself into habitually stifling your anger, blow the lid off once in a while and see how it feels. If your style has been to explode, try to describe accurately what you feel. Strongly consider staying current with your anger—that is, consciously choose a response to it *as you experience it.* From my experience, hanging on to anger causes far more damage to people and their relationships than does its rapid, respectful release. Play. Play with options. Notice how you tend to handle little irritations. Then, from time to time, whenever you're a little irritated or even outraged, try a new style of managing the feelings, remembering that there is no universal rule about the right way to do it. This is your life. It's your choice. Don't make a new rule. Just expand your repertoire.

Conflictive situations engender a range of emotions: anger, sadness, sexual feeling, fear, and even joy. Conflict can be vibrant and is part of being fully human. Sometimes it hurts. Sometimes it's a drag. But it does represent an exciting opportunity for personal and interpersonal growth. Poorly handled or left unattended, it will so shield the love inside of you that you will eventually start feeling like you're made out of tin. Handled with guts, respect, love, and finesse, it can lead you into an unabashed plunge back into the feelings of pleasure, harmony, and productivity you really want.

13

RESOLVE CONFLICT: FACE YOUR FOES

Interpersonal conflict is a pain in the neck set off by other people less fair, sensitive, and wise than you and me. But until they shape up and conform to our scripts, let's indulge their insecurities and settle unpleasant matters swiftly so we can all get back to the business of enjoying our lives.

Let's say you find yourself in a thorny conflictive situation. You don't like the way you're feeling; you're considering broaching the issue with the other party involved, but you're nervous about it. What should you do? Well, you know by now that I'm not big on hard, fast rules, but here are some points to ponder:

1. Conflict is made hardest when we feel our act is attacked. Let someone you value imply overtly or covertly that you are less wise, angelic, talented, or thrilling than you would like to think, and you'll sure as shootin' want to deny or correct their skewed perception. Your style may be to disqualify them in your mind, to bully them with blows or bellows, to out-articulate them, to pout, or to work it out. If the latter is your desire, it's important to step out from behind your act and live the truth—at least for a while. To do so, you first have to be honest with yourself about your act. Just ask yourself, "How am I wanting this person to see me and why do I give a damn?'' Consider telling the person your answer to this question. Consider, too, asking the person how he or she is perceiving you. If this person's perception is different from yours, ask yourself and the other person what you have done to inspire such an opinion and reflect on the answers you get. This is the easy part. It's the part where you get to learn about what you're putting out. It can help you make a clear decision to shore up or drop your act prior to leaping off into the next few steps—which are a little tougher and require more guts, but are important.

2. Ask yourself what your motivation is for even considering raising the issue with the other party. Take a good look at your intention to see if it's worth your effort. A good test is to consider stating your intention aloud to the person with whom you are in conflict. If your intention is too low-down or embarrassing to go public with, then your motivation is probably too self-serving to lead to intimacy or to an experience of pleasure, so you probably would be best served to stuff it. If you decide to proceed, express yourself in a way that is consistent with your intention. If, for example, you want to work through a conflict toward a better relationship with someone, say that to the person and go no further until the two of you have established this as your mutual intention.

By the same token, if all you want is to dump some negative feelings or prove yourself right and the other person wrong, be honest with yourself about your agenda and don't pretend otherwise. It's fine to express yourself for the sole intention of getting something off your chest. In fact, it's commendable at times. But be honest about it. If this is your intention, however, make certain that you proceed with respect for people and their belongings, remembering that you are as transparent as the rest of us and to simply vent feelings under the pretension of working things out will likely result in your coming off as a phony—a mean phony.

If, having taken an honest look at your intention, you discover that it is to work through the conflict to the point of new clarity and a good feeling between you and the other person involved, following are some further tips to consider.

3. Go slow. Breathe. Relax.

4. If you are fearful of the possible consequences of openly expressing yourself, look your fear square in the eye and ask yourself what is the worst that can happen. Consider making a statement regarding your fear to the other party in the encounter. You might, for example, try out your version of one or any combination of these statements:

> "You're important to me and I want us to remain friends, *and* there are some things you're doing that are driving me nuts."

> "There is something that I want to discuss with you, but I'm afraid that you will throw a fit."

> "Hear all of what I am saying and really consider it before you respond."

> "I'm angry with you. What is also true is that I respect you and value our relationship."

> "I'd like to speak candidly with you and I'd like our conversation to remain between us."

> "I want to really listen to you and I want you to listen to me."

> "This may be a tough conversation for us because my tendency may be to talk ugly and yours may be to give me that sneer of yours. As we have this conversation, let's make an effort to treat each other with love and respect."

> "I'm hesitant to talk with you about a certain sensitive issue, but I don't like feeling what I'm feeling and would like to clear the air. Are you open to a frank discussion?"

Chances are you are no saint either when it comes to handling conflict, so you might want to ask the other person involved if there is any particular behavior of yours he or she wants you to attend to during the encounter.

5. Concentrate on accurately expressing yourself rather than on controlling the other person's behavior. Trade in your desire to be right for a spirit of adventure. Open up to the possibilities inherent in an unpredictable encounter.

6. Listen more than you talk. There are no two ways about it, resolving a conflict takes time and gentle reflection on what the other person says and on what you really want to say. Set a comfortable tempo for the conversation and care enough to seek clarification of the other person's thoughts and feelings.

If you don't have the time for this sort of qualitative conversation, then you don't have a healthy slice of what it takes to be a first-rate spouse, parent, co-worker, supervisor, supervisee, or friend. Make time. Working through conflict not only can restore harmony in relationships, it can move the relationship to a higher level of functioning, a deeper level of authenticity, and an expanded level of potential productivity.

7. Get in touch with what you feel and think, and express it. Separate what you actually feel and think from what you are telling yourself you *should* feel and think, from what you imagine, and from self-righteous justifications of your opinion. Express yourself accurately, taking ownership of your positive and negative thoughts, preferences, and feelings. Describe your thoughts and feelings as belonging to you and you alone. Describe your experience just as you would a painting or a piece of music. For example:

> "I'm aware of being miffed when I find myself waiting for you."

"I love watching you walk."

"Your voice soothes me."

"I tighten up and have a hard time listening to you
when you're yelling."

"I feel tense around you."

"I like you."

"I feel good when I'm with you."

8. If the conflict unfolding is fueled by an annoying behavior of the other party's, be certain to describe vividly the behavior to that person. Be descriptive but not judgmental. "I hate it when you act like a jerk" is going to be less well received than "I get angry when you interrupt me."

9. Communicate congruently without blaming or being whiny and self-effacing. That is, allow your voice, your facial expression, and your body to accurately convey your feelings. Express yourself fully and completely, both with regard to your feelings and your thoughts, but do so in a manner that respects other living things, their space, and their property. Yell if you must, growl if you must, cry if you want. But don't call people names, hurl curses, pout, or bust up property.

10. Remember where you end and all else begins. If you feel defensive, say so. If you can't for the moment, let go of a desire to win, say so, and suggest a specific time to talk again.

11. Be open to feedback even if it smarts. Almost anything that is said about you is in some way true. Conflict represents an incredible opportunity for personal growth.

12. If it is possible, suggest a solution, but remember that resolving a conflict doesn't always mean coming to an agreement. Sometimes an agreement simply isn't possible. I have been pleasantly and frequently astounded in my nearly twenty years of work with families, couples, and organizations to see how often open expression and wholehearted listening diffuses conflict without any obvious solution being reached.

13. If, after doing an honest character check with yourself, you notice that your true motivation is to be right, to win, or simply to infuriate, try being sassy. An eight-year-old Little Leaguer whose batting stance I was attempting to modify stopped me dead in my tracks with this line: "If you're so smart, why ain't you rich?"

14

CHANGE WITH CHANGE

When I was eighteen, I came within one shot of tequila of having indelibly carved and inked into my right forearm a tattoo of a red serpent wound around a silver saber. Above the design there was to be a waving white banner proudly announcing the era's motto of macho mania,

"Death Before Dishonor"

I'm glad I didn't get it done. It wouldn't have set well with my mother then, or my clients now. I didn't deserve it anyway. I wasn't a Marine and, while I'm not a big advocate of dishonor, in a pinch, for all I know, I'd choose it over death and, pinch or no, I just might choose it over severe pain. This is true today. I guess it wasn't true then. It may not be true tomorrow. I change. I notice I change. Sometimes out of conscious choice, but more often out of a sort of osmosis, following some abrupt turnabout in my perception of myself, of humankind, or of the universal order of all and everything. One of the earliest such shifts, to my recollection, occurred in 1949.

As a youngster, I worshiped cowboys. Not the ones that wore baggy pants and held their pistols with both hands, or worse yet carried no guns at all. No way! My cowboys were lean and keen with jingling spurs and tall boots—with pants legs stuffed neatly in the tops. They had slim hips that were strapped with low-slung holsters—holsters filled with silver six-guns—two, one for each hand. Their six-guns had pearl handles and did noble deeds. They made poppin' sounds and knocked men down—off balconies, sometimes—but they never drew blood. My cowboys rode muscular stallions, straddled smooth saddles with shimmering silver studs, and had lassos on their saddle horns—for dogies (and for outlaws when need be). My cowboys had a fine time saunterin' through the badlands with their sidekicks, outsmartin' desperadoes, and rescuing sweet young things. My cowboys were fast on the draw, straight shooters, fast thinkers, smooth talkers. They never wasted words.

As a boy, I was one of them—in heart, in spirit, and in heroic deeds of the mind. I walked, talked, and dressed like those cowboys, six-guns and all; and someday I was going to join them. I knew it. Someday, I was going to Texas to be a cowboy.

When I was about five I announced this to my big brother, Frank. He told me that I already lived in Texas. How could this be? The Texas I was heading for had big cacti, stampedes, and gunfights. This place had paved streets, Buicks, and Big John and Sparky on the radio. I refused to believe Frank. He had attacked the purpose of my life, and had done so with indifference—or so it seemed.

I walked immediately into the kitchen seeking the wisdom of a higher source. I knew Mother wouldn't lie. She said Frank was right, and told me that I not only lived in Texas, but I was standing well within its borders at that very moment. Shoulders slumped in dismay, I strolled back to Frank. He was reading a comic book. I called him a low-down polecat. He looked up. I stared him down with steady eyes. Then I shot him—with my six-guns. Both of them.

No doubt about it, life has its moments of disillusionment and its disappointments, and you know as well as

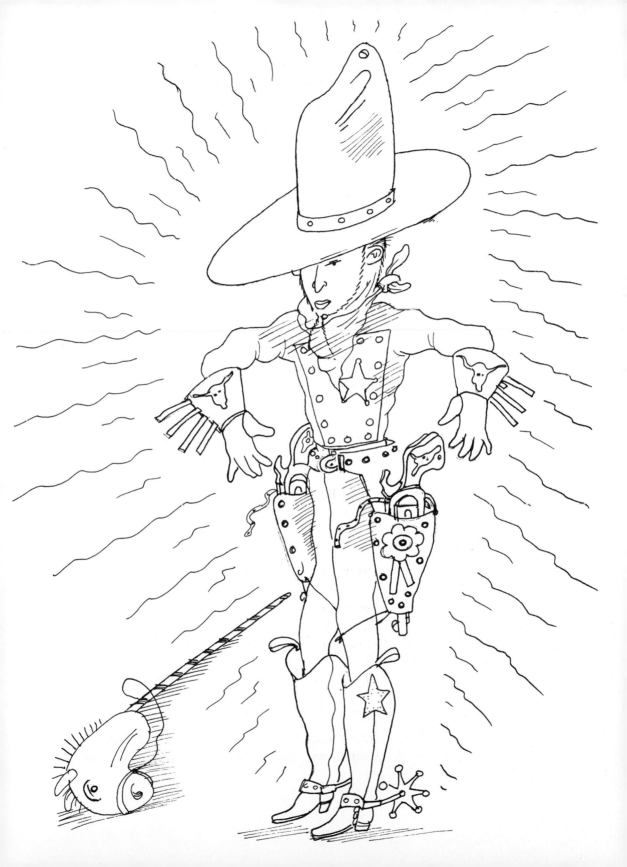

I do that abrupt alterations—especially unpleasant altera-tions—in your props, players, and perceived reality can be very rough. But while a curt, harsh, unceremonious change in personal circumstance or perception can set you on tilt for a spell, you can make the most of it by keeping in mind that life is dynamic and change is inevi-table. Now, I know that sounds like the same sort of banal babble as "put on a happy face" or "buck up," but it's more than a platitude, it's an attitude, and it can be lived.

When some abrupt fit of fate leaves you teetering on the edge between composure and confusion, these guidelines may help you regain your footing:

1. *Ask yourself, "So what?"* Really, "So what?" A change is a crisis only if you perceive it as representing a threat or a loss. What is the perceived loss, if any: a friend, a job, your life, your self-esteem? What is the per-ceived threat, if any?

If you will look closely at your situation when next you find yourself poised on the brink of panic, you will notice that on the most fundamental level you fear aban-donment, pain, or death. It's important to assess how real the threat is. Doing so will help you calm yourself. Sorting out reality (what you know for sure) from fantasy (what you imagine) helps. If you need to gather information in order to distinguish what is real from what you are making up, do so, remembering that it doesn't make good sense to get yourself all worked up over make-believe. There is no positive cause-and-effect relationship between your turning yourself into a nail-biting nervous wreck and your taking constructive action. *Assess, by virtue of whatever critical event has occurred, what has actually been lost or threatened. Then again, ask yourself, "So what?" Get to the bottom line.* If the bottom line is disturbing and you feel action is warranted, do some constructive thinking about what you want to do and do it.

2. In order to successfully move into the realm of constructive thought, you may first need to *take the time*

to experience the emotions conjured up by the event.
You may feel fearful, disappointed, deeply saddened, outrageously angry, or a mixture of all of these. If you've experienced a genuine loss or threat, you may even feel immobilized. Moving through such deep feelings takes time. Lee Doyle, a friend of mine and an exceptionally fine psychotherapist, has a simple but powerful truth on her calling cards:

"Talking About It Helps."

And it can. If you choose to go this route, you may wish to seek out a skilled professional facilitator.

An intensive helper/helpee relationship can be a wondrous and dynamically beneficial process. Skilled facilitators can be found among the ranks of many different professional fields such as social work, psychology, psychiatry, counseling, and the clergy. While specialized training is important, in my estimation the facilitator's professional label is not nearly as critical as how insightful, articulate, and comfortable with himself or herself the facilitator is and how willing you are to let it all hang out in that person's presence. This is a feeling call, and you may have to spend a session or two with him or her to make this determination.

A friend may be the perfect confidant, with whom you can give free rein to your thoughts and feelings regarding your mess of the moment. But if you're feeling devastated, a friend—even a loving, trusted friend—may not be your best resource. This is true for a couple of reasons.

First, a skilled professional facilitator knows where to look, what to look for, and how to intervene effectively toward the goal of helping you open up and express yourself, think through options, re-establish your emotional equilibrium, learn from the experience, and, most importantly, feel better. Besides, on some level, you care what those you really love think about you, so in their presence you are likely to do too much censoring in an attempt to keep them comfortable or to preserve some unspoken agreement about the roles you play in one another's lives. This will in all likelihood be true even with your spouse, your mama, your bosom buddies, and your spit-sisters.

Second, a skilled facilitator is hired help, and with him or her you don't have to give one iota of thought to preserving the relationship or your image. What is more, the whole process is confidential and most of the counselors and therapists I know are quite sincere about helping their clients. They care about their clients and make every effort to create a safe, trusting environment in which their clients can cut loose with emotions and constructively work through feelings and tough situations. If, however, talking about it is absolutely not your bailiwick, don't let that keep you from a full-bodied experience of your thoughts and feelings.

Try stream-of-consciousness writing; throwing a private tantrum complete with wailing, flailing, and hurling curses; pounding a mattress with a tennis racket; or re-watching the saddest movie you've ever seen and having a good cry. To move through a crisis, you must get to the point of constructive thought, and doing so will be difficult until you've taken the time to fully experience your emotional reaction to your dilemma. Doing so may take a few moments or a string of days. The faster and deeper you plunge into and work through your feelings, the quicker you will move to the point of constructive thought.

3. *Remind yourself that worry and constructive thought are entirely different processes.* Worry has little if any value and usually involves going over and over the facts and possible outcomes of your dilemma of the moment until you've created a cerebral house of mirrors. Even if you manage to hit on a solution, if you're in a worry mode, you'll come up with all sorts of objections to the solution. You are, at these points in time, under an all-out siege from your gremlin. Worrying is not fun and it is bad for your health. When next you worry, notice how

it feels. Your breathing will be shallow, your brow will be furrowed, and your body will feel tense in those places your gremlin thinks you are most vulnerable. If you are into less-than-healthy ways of managing your stress such as excessive smoking, drinking, or eating, your gremlin will tempt you with them and then taunt you for following his lead. Your gremlin is not a cute character, or a whimsical concept. Your gremlin is a force within you that is out to destroy you. He can do so by perpetuating worry. The experience of worry is uncomfortable and destructive.

Worry is laced with anxiety and fraught with anguish. It grows out of a preoccupation with fears about the future, an unwillingness to release the past, and/or a refusal to accept what is obvious in the here and now. Constructive thinking, on the other hand, begins with a willingness to look yourself and your situation squarely in the eye. It requires relaxed concentration, the ability to control your awareness, and telling yourself the truth. It is sometimes inspired by anxiety but never dominated by it.

Constructive thinking requires an awareness of where you are and a notion of where you want to be. It entails a review of possible resources, a sensitivity to potential snafus, and at least a rough plan for efficiently using your resources to bound over, circumvent, or bust through the stumbling blocks on your path to situational goal attainment and a renewed sense of cool, calm contentment.

After one of life's smashing upsets, you can restore your balance by separating fact from fantasy, experiencing and getting a perspective on the thoughts and feelings stirred up by the crisis, and doing some constructive thinking and planning. Becoming aware of your skin—that perpetual boundary between you and all else—won't hurt either. Having re-established your balance and the "here and now" as your home base, you can make a choice. Choice is the key to restoring your balance. You might choose to do some constructive thinking, fret yourself into a frenzy, scream, go eat Mexican food, or, impossible as it may seem, fantasize a positive outcome to your situational upset. The latter is a potent strategy. Positive images feel better and are better for you than worry. Images are the language of the mind, and there is a wealth of data to support the idea that the mental images you create and cavort with dictate your future and its quality.

15

RELEASE YOUR OUTDATED CONCEPTS

Your potential for a souped-up, go-get-'em existence is far greater than even your most splendid idea, so it's important to see even marvelously grandiose beliefs about yourself and the world for what they are—concepts.

There's a not-so-old adage that says, "There are two kinds of people in the world—those who think they can and those who think they can't. They're both right." Your concepts influence the quality of your life. The first step in eliminating a counterproductive concept from your consciousness is to become aware of it.

One concept that seems to burden many of the folks with whom I come in contact is "I better not get my hopes up." It usually emerges when one is on the brink of possible good fortune, and I usually hear it expressed as "I'm afraid to get excited." I often ask, "Why?" And just as often the response is, "I'm afraid I'll be disappointed." There is a myth at play here. Its specific origin varies from person to person, but usually it's grounded in a concept that one is undeserving of good fortune or that good fortune only comes after suffering. Too often the net result of this concept is the choice to fill precious moments of one's existence with lukewarm anticipation rather than with delectable excitement. Should you become aware of this tendency within yourself, consider plunging into the excitement. It just may be that allowing yourself to expect the best and to feel the excitement inherent in doing so will create a fertile ground in which good happenings can prosper. Even if the good fortune you anticipate doesn't manifest itself and you feel some disappointment, sadness, or anger, if you dive headlong into these feelings they won't last long. In the meantime you will have relished your excitement for moments or days on end and will have done a prime job with one of your top priorities—enjoying yourself.

Becoming aware of your concepts and your images can be tricky business, since many of your self-limiting notions are buried deep in your unconscious, and you may be unaware of them. You may be wrapped in so tight a clinch with them it's as if you and they are one. You can, however, bring them into your awareness and, with some artful maneuvering and fancy footwork, dance your way out of their grip. You can begin to truly take ownership of your life, developing a style of being and living that is based on your own capabilities, talents, preferences, and desires rather than on those set in place by old ideas formed from past experiences.

The process of becoming aware of your concepts and shedding and/or modifying them is a continuous one, since as you free yourself of antiquated concepts, you will no doubt form new ones, and they, too, will eventually become outdated and limiting. But the process of continued self-awareness can be a rousing escapade in which you live life as a prospector with the natural you as the mother lode. And time already served is not a factor. An old dog can indeed learn new tricks. So whether you're a crusty old pro or a trembling tenderfoot when it comes to taking charge of your life, as long as you can get some distance between you and your limiting beliefs *about* you, you can spice up your personal pleasure, your productivity, *and* your relationships.

I'm going to suggest an exercise to help you with the process of discovering some of the concepts you may be saddling yourself with about you and your potential.

To do this experiment, I suggest you employ a process I call first-level thought.

First-level thought is the simple process of gently reflecting on any given topic during a couple of full, easy, and complete breaths. It is a superior alternative to worrying, and it can at times serve you even better than in-depth constructive thought. While in-depth constructive thought has an important place in your life, there are many times when first-level thought will serve you more efficiently. First-level thought involves trusting your innate ability to come forth with usable information quickly and effortlessly and is especially valuable in learning about yourself and getting in touch with your most fundamental feelings and preferences. First, however, let's take a moment to discuss the process that you and I, at this very moment, are going through together.

I'm enjoying writing this book. I hope that you're enjoying reading it. I suppose it's possible, however, that you're not. You may be bored or confused. If you're bored, I suggest you stop reading for a while. Take a break. You deserve it and there is no need to push on. Becoming better at enjoying your unique and wonderful self is a never-ending process, a process that in itself can be a treat. Travel at a pace that pleases you.

If you're confused, consider the notion that your confusion may be the result of trying to fit what I'm saying into your preconceived notions about what I'm saying. If you're going to read on, relax and enjoy the process, remembering that there is a difference between effort and strain. Effort is required in our work together. Strain is neither required nor beneficial. Your conscious mind doesn't have to understand or agree with what you're learning or relearning in order for you to benefit. Relax. Trust the natural you to integrate what it can use and to eliminate what doesn't fit. Unlike your conscious mind, the natural you doesn't need to work hard, figure out, or analyze in order to make the most of that which will benefit you. But your gremlin, nasty skunk that he is, will do all in his power to convince you that the natural you is untrustworthy. Your gremlin will want you to question, scrutinize, analyze, and dissect all that you read, including the items that follow and your responses to them. Believe me, he has no trust in the natural you. But I do. And you will too, as you begin to make enjoying yourself a top priority, relax, center yourself, and simply notice you, your props, and your players.

The following fill-in-the-blank items will help you become aware of some of the concepts of yourself that you may be carrying around. Use first-level thought in responding to them. Simply take a couple of full, clear breaths while allowing your mind to focus on each item. Don't fret or strain or analyze or work hard to come up with a "just right" answer. Trust your first-level thought. Your answers are between you and you, and need only be true for you here and now. Be honest. Honesty in this activity will help you shape up. You need to be settled down and relaxed to give this activity your best shot. Remember what you've learned about choice, and if you're not enthusiastic about responding to these items now, don't. When you're ready, get some paper and something to write with and dive into the experience.

- I am incredibly _____ _____.
- I am a lousy _____.
- I am _____ intelligent.
- I have a knack for _____.
- I am extremely good at _____.
- I am a(n) _____ athlete.
- Most folks who really know me think that I am

  _____.
- I will never learn to _____.
- I am a run-of-the-mill _____.

Stick with what comes up first. Don't argue with it, just note it and jot it down. Every answer you are jotting down is an idea. That is all—an idea, a concept, a belief, an image, an intangible bit of hullabaloo. *But* it's an intangible bit of hullabaloo that is powerfully hypnotic, and if it's left to lie unnoticed in your unconsciousness, it will permeate your experience and dictate your future. The images in your mind predispose your reactions to your experiences in life. All hypnosis is self-hypnosis, and self-hypnosis is as constant and perpetual a process for human beings as is breathing. So if your desire is to become an exemplary player at the game table of life, it's time to straighten up, fly right, and give yourself a fair and square shot at being the best you can be and at having the best time you can have. A shot based on who you are now—not on who you decided to be in the olden days. Your responses on the items just given and those that follow will give you some important clues as to how you may be limiting or aiding your pleasure and productivity. Let's continue now.

- My life is _____.
- My future is going to be _____.
- I would rather be _____.
- I am far too _____.

Come on, be honest. It's more important to trust your first-level thought than to paint a nice picture.

- As a lover, I am _____.
- My body is _____.
- My health is _____.
- I am _____ to look at.
- I am _____ prosperous.

You are greatly influenced by the self-concepts you carry in your head. Strive to become aware of your self-concepts. By consciously throwing some out, modifying others, and forming new ones, you can become the over-seer, the soothsayer, and a loving guide of your own life.

There are several ways you can experiment with actively shedding or changing outdated ideas you've been lugging around. Among them are simply noticing, playing with options, redesigning, and re-experiencing.

16

SIMPLY NOTICE AND PLAY WITH OPTIONS

By bringing prevalent beliefs about yourself into the foreground of your conscious mind as you've just done, you've already begun to lessen their impact on you. Easy, huh? But true. There is a theory of positive personal growth at work here—a theory that has been around for thousands of years. I elaborated on it in *Taming Your Gremlin* and I think it's important enough to be restated here. Here's my version of the theory:

> I change for the better, not by trying to be
> different than I am, but rather by becoming fully
> aware of how I've been tripping myself up.

I've heard this referred to as the Zen Theory of Change, the Existential Theory of Change, the Gestalt Theory of Change, and the Paradoxical Theory of Change. Lao-tzu, who lived over four thousand years ago, spread his wisdom in Chinese, but here's an English translation of a few of his words:

> "Observe the natural order and work with it
> rather than against it, for to try to change what is
> only sets up resistance."

This wisdom can be a powerful tool in expanding your personal pleasure and power. Use your powers of observation and trust the natural you to make use of what is observed, especially regarding beliefs you hold about yourself, your life, and the world. This theory of change becomes an especially potent experiential aid to self-enhancement when you *simply notice* your self-limiting concepts *as they are playing through your head in real-life situations.*

I hang my head in shame that on one item in the exercise in Chapter 15 my first-level thought was, "I am far too *covetous.*" "Of what?" you might ask. Of damn near anything someone else has that I want, including but not limited to a mint-condition 1957 Chevrolet hardtop, six-foot-four stature, and thick hair. I'm afraid it's been so, and while I want to think I'm too smooth to show it, I have a hunch it's a quality that's about as subtle as a neon sign. Here's how it has worked—until now. If you have it and I want it, my tendency has been to get mad at you (but probably not show it). This is in spite of the fact that I am loving, well-mannered, and true blue. Like my craving for semi-sweet chocolate, my covetous nature seems fundamental to my being. But because I'm aware of this undistinguished quality of my personhood, I now have at least a modicum of power when it comes to choosing how to respond to it. I won't snarl, get in your face, and scream *"Giveittume!"* I won't talk bad about you. I won't hurl curses at you or call you a dirty name. And I won't fake a smile, touch your arm gently, and murmur, "I'm so happy for you." In fact, I don't know what I will do from this point forward with my tendency to be covetous. But simply by virtue of describing it to you, I will be more aware of it and will be more at choice when it comes to choosing a behavior in response to it.

Every time you simply notice one of your mind's less-than-positive tapes, especially if you do so *as the tape is playing,* you can attend to it with a sense of relaxed detachment, even with humor, and you can be at choice with your reaction. This gives the natural you a chance to check out the tape's value in the context of the present situation. You needn't strain to change, or waste time delving into your past to ferret out the tape's origin. Just relax and place your awareness on the message. Really attend to it. Turn up the volume on it for a few moments. Hear it, but don't take it too seriously. Do this on a few occasions, and before long the message on the tape, if it is untrue, maladaptive, or simply no longer beneficial to you, will begin to fade in intensity.

Your gremlin will attack you with fear tactics in the form of catastrophic expectations and painful memories in an effort to keep self-limiting messages and behaviors in place. Follow his lead and you'll feel blah (from repeating the same behaviors over and over again), blue (from feeling like no one knows the real you), or bottled up (from overcensoring true expressions of yourself).

The natural you, on the other hand, is masterful at modifying counterproductive thoughts and traits once you bring them and your gremlin's wailing out of the shadows. The brighter the light you shine on old fears, outdated ideas, and cumbersome habitual behaviors, the better the natural you can see the absurdity in them.

To have some fun exposing antiquated notions and beliefs, think of ways to accent them. Let's imagine, for example, that at the close of a board meeting in which you had given what you thought was an exceptionally fine stand-up presentation, you discovered that you had done the entire presentation dragging a piece of toilet paper around on your shoe. And let's say your gremlin calls you an unthinking buffoon and chides you with put-downs. Instead of trying to turn off his chatter, give him a microphone. Listen to him for a time-limited period. Imagine a vicious tirade spewing from his mouth.

"You idiot. Now they'll know you aren't perfect. They'll know you have bowel movements and, worse yet, that you haven't mastered the process of cleaning yourself up afterward.

What's-His-Face probably thinks you are incompetent, and Old-So-And-So sure as hell has dropped any idea that you're an attractive human. They're all probably snickering about you right now. You're as good as out of a job. You'll be walking the streets. You'll have to sleep under a cardboard box (if they're not all taken). And you'll probably get beaten up, and survive, but you'll be brain dead. Or maybe you'll just starve on the streets. I knew you'd blow it. I knew it. You never deserved to be on the board anyway. You've been bluffing. You're an imposter. The jig's up, Babycakes."

Fritz Perls, a truly brilliant psychiatrist and teacher, was a whiz when it came to accenting the obvious. In his psychotherapeutic method he frequently accented the obvious to the point of absurdity, bringing vividly into the consciousness of his patients precisely how they were interrupting their pure experience of themselves and of their lives. Woven through the fabric of his approach was a knowledge of experimental psychology, psychoanalytic theory, human behavior, existential philosophy, and anatomy and physiology. His approach was efficient and effective, primarily because it was existential—dealing with the client's experience in the here and now; phenomenological—leading people to observe and experience *how* they tended to feel, think, and behave rather than *why;* and experiential—vividly accenting the client's habitual behaviors, and the concepts on which they were based, so that they could be felt and observed with an attitude of "creative indifference." Fritz Perls was one of several pioneers who developed the potent psychotherapeutic approach known today as Gestalt therapy.

You can use the same sort of existential, experiential, phenomenological approach that Fritz Perls used to

81

enhance your own life. To do so, simply notice and accent the obvious—to the point of absurdity if you wish. Experiment with forming a mental picture of yourself acting out your feelings. If, for example, you observe yourself shrinking from a conflict or hiding from a challenge, try forming a mental picture of yourself acting out your feelings. Imagine yourself growing smaller and smaller, or trembling with fear, or hiding and cowering in a dark closet. Or, better yet—if the situation affords you the opportunity—actually scrunch up your posture, or put your head down, or go hide in a closet, or walk like you have your tail between your legs. Give the natural you the chance to observe the strange behavior and the belief on which it is based.

Be creative and playful with the process of accenting the obvious. If, for example, you notice yourself holding your anger in to the point where you feel like a thundercloud, accent the feeling. Hold your breath, puff up real big, then go look at yourself in the mirror. And don't overlook one of the simplest ways to accent the obvious— that is, to verbally describe to someone else in the present moment what you are noticing about yourself, *as you are noticing it.* Say, for example,

> "I'm really filled with fury right now and I feel myself holding it all inside and puffing up like a thundercloud."

Simply noticing and accenting the obvious can help you in a myriad of situations, but just to get you rolling, consider opting for the following strategies when you next find yourself in a snit.

Simply noticing the message your gremlin is sending your way *as it is playing* gives you some distance, not just from the message, but from that monster of the mind—your very own personal gremlin. Your gremlin is not just the self-limiting messages in your head. *He's the force that brings them forth.* He has a purpose—your

demise—and he moves with forthright intention. Your gremlin is the macabre master of misery, the demon of distress. He will use the data in your mental storehouse to squelch your potential for pleasure and productivity, to weaken your body, and to poison your relationships. But you've got him whipped. Completely whipped. Not once and for all, but in each unique situation in which he flares up and snarls at you. All you have to do is simply notice him with a sense of detachment, accent what is so, and play with options.

As you become aware of your outdated beliefs, you will notice that based on them you have formed habitual ways of responding to feelings and to people. In Chapter 14 we discussed the process of playing with options when responding to the anger sometimes brought forth by interpersonal conflicts. During your many moons on this twirling sphere, you have developed habits for responding to other emotions as well. Emotions such as sadness, joy, and sexual feeling.

I've met folks who, once they started to attend to the chatter in their heads, discovered that they had the expression of uncensored joy confused with irresponsibility and immaturity, and had the rich, full expression of sadness confused with weakness and overdependency. I even had one client who, upon tuning in to her gremlin, heard it mutter,

> "Sex is nasty and sinful . . . and you should save it for the one you love."

Your gremlin is a trickster and not above using confusion as a means of wiping out your chances for simple contentment.

You can have a big time noticing the messages that fly through your mind and by playing with options for expression. Again, don't tell yourself that you should change or must change. Change just for a change. *Play* with options. You'll be wise not to give yourself new rules.

The key to successful gremlin taming is *choice.*

I suggest that you briefly and lightly review your notes from the fill-in-the blank items you completed. Remind yourself of your power to simply notice and to accent the obvious and, of course, of your choice to change just for a change. Then consider tossing (respectfully, I trust) me and *Never Get A Tattoo* aside for a spell. In the fill-in-the-blank activity you've just done, you've generated a great deal of data. The material generated may or may not be new to you, but now that you've brought it or rebrought it into the foreground of your experience, you will be best served to just let it perk for a while. If you want to do some gentle self-reflection, enjoy the process and don't get heavy about it. When it comes to gremlin taming, contrary to the sign in your high school locker room, there is no gain in pain (or strain). I've got a couple more methods of releasing old concepts in store for you. I'm sure they'll help you if you'll give them sincere consideration, and you'll be more likely to do so if you're fresh as a daisy.

Go Be.

17

JUST IMAGINE IT
[REDESIGNING]

There is a great deal of emphasis nowadays on the belief, or at least the possibility, that if you can imagine it, you can have it.

It's a lie. At least it's not true from my experience, and I've given the theory a first-class run for its money. This is not to say that positive visualization cannot do wonders in your life. It can. I, for one, have benefited from and appreciate the work and wisdom of Bernie Siegel as reported in his book *Love, Medicine, and Miracles,* and the work of other pioneers in the field of creative visualization such as Shakti Gawain. But as for me, I tend to run headlong into limits—maybe because I believe there are limits. I'm not sure. A former client of mine named Joann described the dilemma aptly.

Joann and her husband, Glen, were deeply involved not just with one another but with an organization to which they belonged. The organization sponsored an ongoing series of personal growth seminars which Joann and Glen attended weekly. Some of these were evening events and others were workshops that lasted from Friday night through Sunday. Joann and Glen continued to participate in these events throughout my work with them and did, I think, some very positive and growth-producing visualization work. As individuals they were expanding their boundaries (and their jargon), but circumstances in their marriage were still far less than rosy. In one of our sessions, Joann expressed her fear that their marriage would fall apart, to which Glen replied, "Joann, if you hold in your mind that our marriage will fall apart, our marriage will fall apart." Joann looked at Glen calmly and then asked simply, "Well, Glen, if I hold in my mind that our dog will shit gold nuggets, will it?"

Joann has a way with words, and I offer these particular ones to you simply as a way of saying that, while in my opinion creative visualization is among the most exciting tools you and I have for promoting positive change in our lives, it's a good idea to balance it with some constructive thought, some hard work, and some good choices.

From my experience, it is absolutely true that people whose lives are filled with love, prosperity, and contentment are people who see in their mind's eye and believe in their hearts that their lives will evolve positively and that they deserve the best life has to offer. These folks, however, also tend to be people who like and respect themselves and who are willing to take the time and make the effort to plan constructively and do the work necessary to get them where they want to be.

If you plan your steps out carefully to get from point A to point B, and if your steps are realistic, and if you put one foot in front of the other, you will, in all likelihood, get where you want to go. When I help my clients with the process of bringing about constructive changes in their lives, I focus with them on breaking antiquated, self-limiting concepts of who they are and what they can accomplish. I focus with them on forming new concepts (here's where creative visualization comes in), on planning, and on doing.

Modifying and in some cases throwing away deep-rooted but outdated concepts is a challenging undertaking because it is so personal a process and because it has to go on right inside your very own cranium. No one can

do it for you. So far we've discussed two surefire tactics you can use together quite well: simply noticing (including accenting the obvious) and playing with options. Following is another. It's a more aggressive approach and is best used in conjunction with the others. I call it redesigning.

Review your responses to the fill-in-the-blank items you completed earlier, and isolate those items you see as having a less than positive influence on you in your life. Play with rewriting them in the form of ultrapositive affirmations. Imagine that you are creating for yourself a script for a subliminal tape that is going to be used in your own self-hypnosis. Don't be shy about plugging in responses that make your life seem finer than you've ever before dreamed possible. Do so, even if it feels like you're telling yourself a bundle of outrageous, self-glorifying lies. Elaborate and do so in your own words. This is a very personal and private process and a very powerful one, so milk it for all it's worth. You can use what you write as the basis for an internal program designed to fill your life with more pleasure and less pain than you heretofore thought likely. You can do it! And it's well worth the effort.

For example, on the third item, if you originally wrote "I am *fairly* intelligent," you might now write, "I am smart as a whip and quick-witted to boot. I get a real kick out of how quickly I learn. It's a blast to be fast." Do this sort of reworking with all of the items to which your responses were obviously self-limiting, and use the information you draft as a basis for a rap with Old Number One. Trot it out and say it loud and proud *every chance you get.* In your rewriting, use words that fit for you rather than rote declarations. I find, and my clients have supported this notion, that going on a positive tirade in your head is more fun and produces more rapid qualitative results than one-sentence affirmations such as "I am very intelligent" or "I am loving and wise." Get into the process. Be indulgent. Where positive self-talk is concerned, restraint is a bad idea. Go on for moments on end if you choose.

With the issue of intelligence, for example, don't merely tell yourself that you will become intelligent, but rather that you are already brilliant, that at this moment you are becoming more so, that the process will continue, that you deserve to grow wiser, and that it is a done deal that is right now manifesting and pervading every aspect of your life. You can do the same with remarkable results regarding your sex appeal, your lovability, your likability, your relationships, your health, and even your income. Do it.

And don't be namby-pamby about it. Embellish the process by creating images of yourself feeling and being exactly as you would like and of your life working just the way you want it to. Be unrelenting. Create positive images, then conjure them up and give them a concentrated look-see every chance you get. If my haranguing and prodding fall short of motivating you, you might want to familiarize yourself with some of the material on positive visualization reported in the health care field alone. There are many such works. Among those I heartily recommend are *Love, Medicine, and Miracles,* by Bernie Siegel, and *Getting Well Again,* by Carl and Stephanie Simonton and James Creighton. The work they have done using positive visualization with cancer patients is inspiring and heartwarming.

Now, I know that stick-in-the-mud gremlin of yours thinks this power of positive thinking stuff is all a bunch of frothy guff. But if your self-awareness is up to snuff, you'll notice that listening to your gremlin feels a helluva lot worse than affirmative self-talk and positive visualization, and it's a darn sight worse for you. Shattering old concepts and replacing them with affirmative inner talk and images toward the goal of sweetening your very own life not only feels good, it's good for you, and *used in conjunction with common-sense planning and doing, it can make for a noble transformation.*

Settle into some affirmative heart-to-hearts with yourself, if only briefly, each day for three weeks. Center yourself and then give the process a wholehearted go. Even if it feels like pounds of phony-baloney for a few seconds at the beginning of each stint, just stick with it. Soon you will feel yourself settle into the experience. Consider the three-week period a test run and check out the results. If the process starts feeling like homework, drop it for a while. When you're ready, pick up the challenge and get into it. Notice not just the long-term effects, but the pleasure that emerges as you dabble with the process. Notice, too, the true love that is the essence of that pleasure, and enjoy it.

18

PLAN AND DO

Here's a simple formula for accomplishing or producing something: Know what you want to accomplish. Write down the steps necessary to get it done. Set a date for gracefully taking each step. Be willing to change the dates without giving up the project. Take the steps.

When it comes to planning and doing, some folks are great at seeing the big picture—a fantasy of how it could be—but have difficulty in attending to detail. This may work for you if you are rolling in dough or are such a shining star that you can demand the time, devotion, and effort of top-notch detail people. For most of us, however, it's important to remember that dreaming comes easy and that the chasm between big ideas and a high-quality, finished product is deep and wide. You can bridge it by laying across it two long parallel planks—*purpose* and *confidence*—and by affixing to the planks some logical, sequential, goal-oriented steps. *Purpose* springs from desire, and the best desire springs from your heart. *Confidence* is the result of giving something—anything—your best butt-kickin' effort and seeing it manifest in your favor.

I've had people say to me about projects they've considered taking on, "I'd try it, but I just don't have the confidence." It's a screwy outlook. It implies somehow that confidence is like dandruff or measles—that it just sort of hits you or doesn't. Not so. Confidence is more like a set of rippling abdominals: you have to put out to gain it. To say "I can't do it because I don't have the confidence" is putting the cart before the horse. You build confidence by taking risks—calculated risks based on underpinnings of self-respect, realism, and a willingness to see and accept imperfect starts as part of the process leading to goal attainment.

H. Stephen Glenn, a fine writer and teacher, tells a story about Jonas Salk. Dr. Glenn points out that Dr. Salk, in the process of discovering the polio vaccine, conducted over two hundred formal experiments. When asked by an interviewer how he felt about those two hundred failures, Dr. Salk pointed out to the interviewer that he couldn't identify with the word *failure*. He explained that to him, each experiment was an important part of the trial-and-error process of accomplishing what he wanted to accomplish. Thank goodness Jonas stuck with it. Polio in its time was as great a threat as the AIDS virus is today, and thanks to his persistence we've got polio under control.

As you and I try to influence our destiny, we are sure, from time to time, to get so caught up in dreaming about our destination or so distracted from it that we take an occasional fall. But while we're sprawled out on the ground, let's pick something up. A piece of wisdom, maybe. Then let's pull ourselves upright, dust ourselves off, and move on with our project.

Creating steps that are manageable in size is wise, too. If you try to build your bridge between where you are and where you're going with steps that are too grandiose or weighty, setting them in place will appear to be such a struggle you may tend to avoid trying it.

By the same token, don't overdo on the detail work. It's okay for your bridge to look spiffy, but if you get hung up chiseling and sanding each plank into a master woodcrafter's work of art, you may grow feeble before you get the bridge built and you across it. This may not be a bad way to spend time if it keeps you happy, but if you think you'll be even happier once it's built, you'll be better served to keep moving and to keep your focus.

Staying focused requires conscious intent. I emphasized earlier that your awareness is a spotlight that you control. It is. But sometimes the props and players in your world may jump up and down, yell at you, or sing and do a tap dance trying to get you to shine your light on them instead of on the project at hand. If they are important to you, make time to do so. Structure your day so that when possible you consciously select where you want to focus your beam of awareness, how broadly and brightly, and for how long. Staying centered will help you stay focused, as will positive visualization, simply noticing, playing with options, remembering where you end and all else begins, and asking for help even if your gremlin objects. So will taking enough breaks from your project to keep you from burning out.

You now have a small arsenal of arms for zapping the whips and scorns of time, circumstance, and psyche. These are simply noticing (including accenting the obvious), playing with options, planning, doing, and redesigning. Let me offer you one more arrow for your quiver.

The restrictive concepts that may have emerged in the fill-in-the blank activity you did in Chapter 15 came from out of your own mental storehouse. How on earth did they get in there? While knowing the origin of such beliefs and their resulting behaviors is not always a necessary part of positive change, sometimes it is interesting and helpful.

19

RE-EXPERIENCING

If you take a good look at your concepts and reflect on their origins, you will probably notice that you have formed your ideas from your trials and errors as you've boogied and bungled through life, from what you were told as a child by those you thought knew more than you, and from what you witnessed in the attitudes and actions of prominent players in your world.

Way back when you were an innocent, eager slip of a pup, your mind thirstily lapped up experiences. You slurped down beliefs and behaviors from the folks you spent the most time observing—mom and dad among them. I hope you had the gift of parents with a wealth of honorable intentions and common sense. But even if they were "the most," being human they probably on occasion trotted out some of their more unflattering traits right before your baby blues. You drank in the less than admirable right along with the terrific day after day. Here's a simple experiment to help you gain some insight into some of the impressions you may have unthinkingly gulped down. Make a list of eight to fifteen words and short phrases that describe the parent with whom you were the most intimate prior to the age of ten. If deciding which parent to use is difficult, flip a coin. You can learn a great deal from doing this with either parent.

Imagine, in doing your list, that your goal is to give me a feeling for the kind of person that parent was when you were a child. You might, using your father for an example, reflect on how he presented himself to the world; what was important to him; how he managed his emotions of anger, joy, and sadness; how he expressed or withheld affection; how physically stroking he was; how he handled difficult situations in his life; any prominent personality characteristics or physical traits he had; something about his value system; and anything else you can imagine would give me a feeling for who he was to you when you were a child.

While the reckless and featherbrained may be tempted to read further now, the wise and pure will read no further before having written his or her list.

Having now done so, look over your list of your parent's characteristics and ask yourself which of the qualities you have written down you have taken on as your own. Be honest with yourself. It doesn't matter if you like the qualities, loathe them, or are indifferent to them—if they fit for you, even a little, place a checkmark beside them.

Look now at those qualities you've checkmarked and ask yourself which ones you'd like to throw in the garbage, and put a minus (−) sign by them; which ones you'd like to keep, enjoy, and perhaps embellish, and put a plus (+) sign by them; and which ones you'd like to make useful for you by modifying or reworking them, and put an X by them.

The latter category (those you placed an X by) may need some clarification. Here's an example: A client of mine, Russell, feels he has inherited his dad's "pushiness." He says he wants to modify this quality by keeping his father's assertiveness and his forthrightness when it came to standing up for himself, but he wants to eliminate the brash insensitivity to others he saw in his dad and sometimes witnesses in himself. By bringing this quality into his awareness and noting it as one he wishes to modify, Russell has already begun to lessen its hypnotic hold on him. To enhance his process of personal growth he can "simply notice" his tendency toward pushiness *as it is occurring* and he can simply notice the concepts playing through his head at those moments. He may, for example, note that he tends to be pushy when he feels vulnerable, or when his "in charge" act is on the line, or when he believes he is going to be hurt or abandoned. He can re-evaluate his behavior and his anxiety-based belief in light of present circumstances. He can accent the obvious, and if he's feeling feisty, he can change just for a change and experiment with modifying the behavior.

Via an intense experiential version of the exercise you've just completed, Sharon, a participant in one of my recent seminars, became quite certain that, while she deeply loved, truly liked, and much admired her mother, she had assimilated from her one particularly disturbing tendency. Sharon became aware that, like her mother, she was often "harried." She tended to overwhelm herself with things to do and to scurry about, feeling anxious, certain she would never complete all that she had to do. Sharon noted that this was most true for her when she was at her office and her workday was drawing to a close. At these times, Sharon's thoughts usually became scattered and rapid, her breathing became shallow and fast, and like her mother, she moved in a fashion she termed as "jerky and quick." Consumed with worry during these times, she became insensitive to what was going on around her and often misplaced things and was unintentionally curt and sometimes downright rude to her co-workers. Sharon discovered that she had incorporated this behavior from observing her mom, who believed that a woman's value was tied solely to the degree of activity she engaged in, and that having too much to do and suffering about it was somehow noble. Sharon told me she wanted to make an effort to give up this behavior, and the concept on which it was based, in its entirety.

I suspect that Sharon will be quite successful at

modifying her tendency toward a helter-skelter mindset. After all, she has already brought it into her awareness, activating the existential theory of change you and I discussed earlier. And she can expedite the change she desires by simply noticing her tendency to scurry about *as the tendency manifests itself in her actual workday.* She can simply notice the I-have-to-produce-to-be-worthwhile tape playing in her head and give it whatever power she chooses. She can accent it if she chooses and she can play with options—options such as modifying her breathing, smoothing out her movements, focusing on one issue at a time, and taking the time to come out of her head long enough to notice her props and players.

You can use the information you have gathered from reflecting on your parent to enrich your life and fashion your style of being. Focus on one characteristic for two or three days. Clearly decide what part you want the characteristic to play in your life. You might decide to embellish it, lessen it, or eliminate it entirely. The keys to effective change using this method are to stay conscious of what part you want the characteristic to have in your life, to simply notice the characteristic as it pops up in your own personality, to be at choice, and to *play* with options. *Play* with making the characteristic bigger, littler, or nonexistent. And keep it all to yourself. It's a personal matter. A secret between you and you. A way to help yourself to a bit of you. An inner sport.

If you have a characteristic you really want to doll up or dampen, you might do well to include it in your practice of positive visualization and positive self-talk. Your primary motive is to expand the space between you and the characteristic so that you can view it with a sense of detachment and gain the free will to do some creative choreography with your own personality and performance.

Keep in mind that your very own confining, negative, and/or outdated concepts and behaviors come from a massive makeup of folks and factors, so for heaven's sake don't waste time seeking out someone to blame—least of all your parents. Parents are easy targets and too often they get a bad rap they don't deserve. Most parents I've met try their darnedest to do right by their kids, and while I'm not sure about your parents' intentions or actions, I know for certain that if you cling to the belief that your shortcomings are their fault or, sillier yet, their responsibility, you won't sink all the way into the fulfillment and contentment you deserve.

As you practice simply noticing, playing with options, tossing out old concepts, and creating new ones, you will learn or relearn, perhaps on a deeper level than before, that you are in charge of your life. It's true. Like it or not, you are in charge. If that realization has not left you shaking in your shoes, you have not fully had it.

One way or another, we all at some point get hit in the face by a blast of wind, open our eyes, and see that we are not only on the bow of a colossal ship on an open sea, but that we're the captain of the damn thing. Once you glimpse this fact of life, you have some choices. You can squeeze your eyes shut and make believe you don't have to take the wheel, or you can run around flapping your arms and yelling, "Somebody take the wheel! Somebody take the wheel!" Or you can take the wheel and learn to handle it. If you settle down and trust the wind instead of fearing it, you'll eventually become pretty good at sailing. You will find that while you don't know what's around the next cape, and while you may at times work up a soaking sweat trying to stay afloat in a nasty storm, all in all you can have a fine time sailing where you want to, and occasionally you can drop anchor and bask in the sun. The breeze is always blowing, at least a bit, so keep your sails unfurled.

What you do with your life is up to you. It's not up to your mom, your dad, your spouse, your pals, your clergyman, or your therapist. It's all up to you. And just underneath the fear of being in command of your life is excitement about being in command of it. Best of all is the freedom—the freedom to lead your life your way, testing the waters on your own, getting your very own battle scars, and relishing your own rewards. You may hook up with a sidekick or two on this sea of life, but even those relationships will work best if each of you has a clear sense of ownership of your own life.

20

SET YOUR INTERNAL METRONOME

Sharon is still on my mind, probably because her di-
lemma-of-the-day was one version of a struggle I see so
many otherwise clear-headed people having. I'm going
to leap to the punch line:

> There is no positive cause-and-effect correlation
> between being harried and getting a job done
> expediently and effectively.

Being harried is a game. It is an act and it has a
payoff that appears positive but in the long run can be a
drag on the disposition and productivity of its player and
a pain in the ass for the folks with whom that person
comes into contact. People who play harried do so as a
way of announcing to others and proving to themselves
that they are worthy and noble, as demonstrated by their
willingness to suffer; and that others in the world have no
right to be upset with them, as demonstrated by the fact
they are trying so very hard; and that screw-ups are not
their fault, as demonstrated by the fact that "No one could
possibly straighten out this mess or get all of this done."
Some folks are professionals at playing harried. The rest
of us are harried on occasion in spite of knowing better.
When *you* feel hassled and harried, your breathing

102

is shallow and fast, your heartbeat is rapid, you perspire if only slightly, you look coyote-eyed, and you feel like gnawing on leather. When habitual hard-core harriedites do it, they too look frantic, but with a forlorn, pitiful tint.

To modify your own occasional fits of frenetic fervor, first catch yourself in the act and ask yourself, "What, Dear One, are you trying to prove?" Then relax your breathing, take in all of the air that you want, and exhale fully—and then set your internal metronome. Here's how.

Think of your breathing as a metronome that you can use to regulate your psychic tempo. Your challenge is to set the metronome at a tempo that allows you to accomplish whatever you want to accomplish at the speed you want to accomplish it, while still "breathing easy." You can use your metronome to set a pace for activities as physically demanding as competitive cycling or running, or for intensely intellectually demanding activities such as mastering your Rubik's Cube.

To experiment with getting a feel for how to set your pace, I suggest that you first think of an activity you want to perform without getting harried. Use your dominant hand to draw a sideways figure eight in the air. Like this:

The sideways figure eight should be about chest high and a little wider than the width of your shoulders from tip to tip. Do it over and over again in the air in a continuous motion. (Don't try this while holding a glass of V-8 and wearing your favorite T-shirt.) As you make your figure eight, experiment with different speeds of doing so. Find a speed that is compatible with the pace you must travel to comfortably and expediently complete whatever task you have in mind. Once you are satisfied that the pace your hand is traveling matches the pace at which you realistically expect to perform the task, experiment with matching your breathing to the tempo of your hand's movement—making sure to take in all of the air that you want (without hyperventilating) and to exhale fully. You needn't take one complete breath for each completed figure eight. In fact, you probably won't, but if you experiment you will find a breathing tempo that is in harmony with the movement of your hand. Experiment with applying this tempo to the task you have in mind, and as you actually perform the task keep your breathing at the pace on which you've decided. Think in terms of graceful, smooth movements as you perform the task, instead of rapid, jerky ones.

21

LET UP WITHOUT
LETTING YOURSELF DOWN

Don't do what Jimmy Butler did. Jimmy Butler was on my flag football team when we were fifth graders at Overland Elementary. Our coach, Mr. Tirrell, knew that the keys to turning the Overland Oxens into a winning squad were speed and inspiration. He attempted to ensure the latter by calling us "men," letting us put black gunk under our eyes, and telling us daily that "it's not the size of the dog in the fight, it's the size of the fight in the dog." Jimmy Butler and I had total faith in Mr. Tirrell (though our faith took a minor dip the day he bellowed at the top of his lungs, "All right men, pair off in threes"). To get us up to snuff on the speed thing, Mr. Tirrell used to shout simply "Go! Go! Go!" and wave his arm over his head in a circular motion. With this cue, we screamed "Oxens! Oxens! Oxens!" and started running around the football field. We did this every day of the season and, miraculously, most of us got faster. We developed our own methods of running. I learned to run on the balls of my feet and Lee Jason, our quick and feisty quarterback, unclenched his fists when he ran, pointing his fingers out like karate guys do nowadays. He said it helped him to cut the wind. Jimmy Butler's approach to becoming a speedster was to stomp the ground fast and hard as he ran. The intensity of Jimmy's stomps increased in direct

proportion to his ever-heightening desire to run faster. He huffed, puffed, and sweated with undaunted zeal. His desire was inspiring but his pace remained deplorable. The harder he stomped, the slower he got. Having witnessed Jimmy's frustration and that of others since, I'm sure—just as sure as I'm sittin' here—that you can't run faster by stomping the ground harder. Certainly there are times when gutting up comes in handy, but all in all, toil dominated by tension is bad for your health and your disposition and won't help you do a quicker or better job. It may even impede your performance.

22

REMINISCE

Reminiscing is good for you. I've rolled out a few reminiscences in this book. I did so for me and for you. Here's my thinking: It makes me feel good and maybe, just maybe, my doing so will inspire you to do the same, with your friends and your family—your current family and your family of origin. It will help you to get to know one another even better. I encourage—and in some cases insist—that members of most families with which I work do a lot of reminiscing. I call it "story time" and suggest that it take priority over television, house projects, and quarreling. Often I suggest specific, easy-to-follow guidelines, which I will share with you later. While in some instances I suggest that reminiscing be done around a common theme, the main thing is that the person doing the reminiscing simply relax and speak the unrehearsed truth.

I'd like you to experiment with reminiscing. But far be it for me to ask you to do anything I wouldn't do, so first I'll share a fresh reminiscence. For me, honest reminiscing comes easiest if I begin by simply stating something that I'm thinking or feeling at the moment. My theme of thought right now, and in most of my waking moments lately, evolves from my desire to please you, my agent, and my publisher, by writing a book that is both practical and enjoyable. Toward this end I've been reading about writing. This morning I read that "a good writer explodes onto the paper." I'm exploding onto the paper. Whammo! Blammo! Splat! As for me, I admire phrases that imply action, like "he fell bleeding onto the ground" or "his hand found the V of her crotch and pressed against it" or "climb it and twirl" or, the grand-daddy of them all, "they fucked."

"Fuck" was a shoo-in for commanding attention until about twenty years ago, when it was yanked from its hideaway in the dark alleys of men's minds and tossed willy-nilly onto the main street of everyday banal banter. Overexposure hasn't been good for "fuck." Before "fuck" went public, it held a special place in my mind and heart. It was a no-nonsense word. It was sinister and mys-terious and powerful. It implied adventure. Most every-body knew about it, some acted on it, but only the bawdy and irreverent said it aloud. The first time I heard "fuck" I was seven, and my nine-year-old hero, Norman, mum-bled to his snot-nosed, tag-along little sister, Barbara, the words "Go fuck a duck." It made no sense. What was a "fuck"? I felt the impact all the way down to my bones. I'm sure my eyes grew wide and my mouth gaped open. I knew "fuck" was big, bad stuff, but I didn't know what. I asked Norman. He said, "It's when you poke somebody with your peter." I knew about peters (synonyms: tally-wacker, wanger, tater, etc.), but I had heard nothing of poking people with them.

In the next few days I told almost every kid on the block to go fuck a duck. In the midst of a snowball fight with SueAnn and Melissa, the two girls who lived across the street, I bellowed it out at the top of my lungs. Frank, my brother (ten years my senior), heard me, came out, and hauled me into the house. He sat me down and told me not to tell people to go fuck a duck. I could tell he meant business. This intensified the mystery in my mind. That a phrase could warrant a surefire command from my otherwise mild-mannered big brother baffled and thrilled

me all at once. Frank asked me if I knew what "fuck" meant. I said yes. He didn't ask for details or offer new information. I'm glad. If the mental picture I was carrying of "fuck" became any more vivid than "poking someone with your peter," my circuits would have blown sure enough. Frank released me on probation and I went back outside.

The sinister quality of "fuck" has simmered down in my mind since that day thirty-some-odd years ago. But the intrigue and intrinsic power of the word have remained. I respect "fuck" and don't like it tossed around lightly. It's a first-class expletive. It's top-notch and shouldn't be wasted on some small-potatoes dilemma, minor upset, or second-class enemy. "Fuck" is to be savored and, when needed, issued forth with regard for its character. I even hesitate having the word "fuck" appear here. I sincerely want this book to help you, not offend you.

I've just sought counsel. I called a good friend of mine for advice. She's a dignified lady of seventy-five. She's honest, she's always willing to speak her mind, and she never says words like "fuck" and turns off the television when others do. She's my mother. I read her what I've just written. She said, "It's a true story. It makes a point. I hope you use it." My interpretation: If they don't like it, f--- 'em!

When was the first time you heard the word "fuck"? What kind of a question is that, you ask, and why did I pay good money to be asked it? Good question. It's like this. Remembering the first time you heard "fuck" can initiate reminiscing. Now that you and I have taken a surefooted, firmly planted step or two on the path to betterment, I think it's safe to take an honest glance back at the semi-dullards we used to be. It may smart, but if we're playful about it I think it will help us grow. After all, we're all relatively naive souls doing our best to stay cool, calm, collected, and content, and none of us knows enough to stop learning from the rest of us. So let's gut up and go public with a few of our past successes and failures. Maybe if we pool our experience it will, after all, amount to a hill of beans and we'll all leap off into the future a tad wiser and better equipped to create a loving world for ourselves and our kids. Let's reminisce.

So as not to waste your time and mine in frivolous folly, let's make this purposeful by operating within the boundaries of good intention and fair play. These tips will help:

1. Bunch up. Get your body near one or more folks you like. Relax and breathe. Open yourself up to the possibility of pleasure and enhanced potential and then go to the next step.

2. Pick one or more of the items listed in item 7 in this list about which to reminisce. Everyone present can share his or her experience on a common theme; or, if you prefer, select a few items from the list, write them down, separate them, drop them in a hat, and have each person draw one on which to reminisce aloud. If you choose this method, don't draw your topic until your turn to reminisce comes. Otherwise you might be tempted to spend time mentally rehearsing instead of listening to others. If you ask kids to play, and I hope you will from time to time, use some common sense and eliminate those topics you think might be inappropriate.

3. If you are the one doing the reminiscing, go slow. Reflect. Breathe. Begin by making a statement or three about what you're thinking or feeling at the moment, then dive into reminiscing. Give nary a thought to being profound or witty or entertaining. Talk at least three minutes but no more than ten. Steer away from making points about life on planet earth and avoid generalizations. Simply report your experience as you recall it. Allow yourself to remember your thoughts and feelings regarding the event about which you're speaking. Use "I" a lot. Recall the details of your experience—what you saw, what you heard, what you felt, what you thought, even what you were wearing, if you like.

Don't be obsessive about sticking with your topic. Just use it as a starting point, and if, as you get into it, you find your attention drawn to a related memory, follow it and let your mind and mouth ramble.

4. After you have completed your tale, take a moment to reflect on the impact the event had on you. It needn't have blown you out of the water or changed your life. Simply reflect on the impact, whatever it was, and describe it to those present.

5. Now take another moment to share what it was like to tell your tale to those present. For example, comment on what you felt as you began to tell your story and how you felt as you got into it. If you heard your gremlin blowing and going, what did he (or she) say? If you found yourself wanting to impress or entertain, whom were you giving the power to judge you?

6. As you listen to other folks reminisce, relax and enjoy the process. Allow yourself to be fully present by keeping your breathing clear and paying attention—the same sort of attention you would pay to a good movie or to a piece of music. To enjoy a movie, you don't have to try hard. By the same token, you can't be thinking of how you'll pay your taxes or you'll miss the movie. To enjoy a movie, you simply relax and gently cast your awareness on the movie. The same sort of gentle attentiveness is required for good listening. This gives you the chance to learn to use your ears with the same refined proficiency with which most of us have learned to use our mouths.

7. Here are a few topics with which to experiment. You can also have a big time making up your own.

One of the first times you heard the word *fuck.*
Your first romantic kiss.

113

Your adolescence from the vantage point of two or three pairs of shoes you've owned.

Your life as traced through automobiles with which you've had a relationship.

A flirtation you've had.

Your first job.

A time as a preadolescent when you were proud of yourself.

The first time you fell head over heels in love.

A special experience with one of the people present.

An early friendship.

An enemy from your past.

A personal injury or illness you've experienced.

Your circumstances five years ago.

A special time with your dad or mom.

A fight or bitter conflict in your past.

Something you wish you'd done differently.

A time you took a risk.

A personal accomplishment within the last year.

A sad time in your life.

Your teenage idol (or idols) and why you think you selected them.

A joyful time in your life.

Your favorite clothes from the past.

A family gathering.

Acts you've used in your life and how you selected them.

As you dive into this activity, remind yourself of a few of the basics of pleasure:

1. The choice of where to focus your awareness is yours. Among your choices are the pleasure

within you, your props and players, your gremlin's chatter, and various forms of make-believe such as fantasy, memory, worry, rehearsal, or analysis.

2. Your skin is both a sensitive receptor and a boundary. This knowledge is powerful, if you use it.

3. Pleasure is within you. It is a feeling and can be experienced.

4. Proper breathing will help you experience pleasure and consequently love.

5. The essence of pleasure is true love.

6. Your gremlin is out to divert you from the experience of pleasure and of the love that is pleasure's essence. Noticing his chatter without being consumed by it will help you detach from him.

7. You can tame your gremlin on the spot by simply noticing, accenting the obvious if you choose, and playing with options.

8. You can regulate your psychic tempo by setting your internal metronome.

9. You have much to learn and your experience is your best teacher.

10. You have much to teach. Your experience has value to others.

23

FALL INTO LOVE

Reminiscing represents an opportunity to let your natural self come out, frolic about, and cavort with other folks doing the same. It leads to and enhances loving relationships.

Loving relationships are the best kind. They happen when people experience the true love within themselves and when they channel that love to others by listening, talking, and acting in accordance with it.

You can feel the true love within you. True love is the essence of true pleasure, and like pleasure it can be felt within your body. When you next experience pleasure, be it reading a book, strolling in the woods, watching a child play, nibbling your lover's earlobe, or hooting and howling over a Marx Brothers movie, notice not just the stimulus engendering the pleasure but the experience of pleasure itself as it occurs right there within your body. Take one breath's worth of time to appreciate the pleasure and to feel it. Notice the experience of love that is its essence. As you attend to the love, it will expand—slightly, at least. Fall into it! Enjoy it! By focusing on the true love within, enjoying it, and appreciating it, you can sustain it in your awareness.

No description of the experience of true love can glorify it justly. True love is both subtly and powerfully perfect. True love is not a thought (though certainly you can have loving thoughts). True love is an experience. True love is trustworthy, and it exists within you perpetually whether you are attentive to it or not. When it is brought into your awareness by your conscious effort or by an outside stimulus, it will permeate your momentary existence and you will feel content, peaceful, and satisfied. The experience of true love is always available to you, though certainly it is easier to tap into and enjoy under some circumstances than others. Enjoying true love requires intention, above all else. It does not require something or someone to love—though you may feel true love inside yourself in the presence of certain people and things—nor do you ensure yourself a large dose of true love by smiling a lot, talking softly, or hugging people with whom you'd rather just shake hands and say howdy.

As you learn to tap into and enjoy your personal experience of true love, you will become increasingly able to detect what configurations of props and players make it easier to do so. In this way, true love can guide you. When you are in touch with the true love within you, you have the power to move toward experiences that activate and stimulate the love and away from experiences that don't. The true love within you can help you select who to hang out with, what props to surround yourself with, what activities to engage in, and even what and where to eat.

The experience of true love differs from the experience of excitement, sexual feeling, adoration, or desire, though these pleasurable sensations increase in lipsmacking intensity when laced with or founded upon true love. True love is not an emotion, but it underlies many emotions. True love is more fundamental than emotion. True love is not a wave; true love is the water. It provides you with more than gratifying stimulation. True love fulfills you.

Pleasurable stimulation can be thrilling; ask your taste buds or your genitals. But even a first-class titillating tingle remains only stimulation until it awakens the experience of true love lying in a half-sleep behind your heart. Add to a dose of first-class stimulation, one small full-bodied drop of pure love, and you're in for a real treat.

You are hooked on love. So am I. It's a healthy addiction, but if you are not wise to its home within you, you may get hooked instead on whatever external mass of matter or morass of circumstances you imagine to contain it. You can seek true love in a relationship, a bottle of liquor, a refrigerator, or wherever else you imagine it to be, but it's right within you and it will be as long as you live in your body.

Your row to hoe is clearly marked. Dig lightly for love. It's right beneath the surface. It's right there. Breathe on it lightly and, if you drop it, tramp on it, or kick dirt all over it, just dig it out, pick it up, and gently blow the dirt off. True love—the love that sustains you, the love that is you—is indestructible and undamageable. Staying in touch with it and walking, talking, and acting in accordance with it is, however, a challenge. To tap into the true love within you and to stay plugged into it takes intention and relaxed concentration.

I suggest you fall into love each morning. You may wish to develop your own method for doing so. Block out the time, be it five minutes or an hour. If you are weighed down with the blues or if you are anxious or fretful, spend a few moments accenting the obvious and then choose to experiment with accessing the love that exists within you. Centering yourself will help. So will good-feeling memories, positive visualizations, meditation, counting your blessings, being thankful for your life, exercise, making love, or reading the comics. Pro-

vide yourself with a full-bodied dose of pleasure each morning. Once you've created the experience of pleasure, tap into the love that is its essence. Make an effort then to stay hooked up with the love as you charge off into your future.

If you're like me, and you are in many ways, chances are as your day moves along you'll get caught up in the anxiousness of accomplishment, totally forgetting that this gift of love is right inside of you. Remember it is, and you can place your awareness on it and stop wasting energy in pursuit of it. Even if you're basking in an experience of love, you'll still have to pay your bills, do your dishes, and deal with your banker, but having established a fundamental feeling of satisfaction within yourself, your efforts toward your props and players will be less desperate and intense. The rough edges of life will be sanded down. Your relationships, for example, will feel better because you'll be able to enjoy the love you feel within without taxing yourself by struggling to squeeze it out of another person.

If your internal tempo is such that tapping into love seems impossible, you're going too fast. If you're too busy to experience love, then you've bitten off more than you can chew. If you're too caught up in worrying to feel love, then you're thinking too much. If you find yourself so enmeshed in the trips and traumas of your daily life that you lose touch with love, take at least a few breaths of time to reconnect with it.

As for me, I'm grateful that true love is real and exists within me. If all I had to connect with was a belief in love, I would have a terribly hard time. I'm not big on blind faith. But the true love within *is* real, and after I focus on it awhile it becomes more prominent in my awareness. This makes it easier to stay in touch with as I move through the world. And yet, amazing as it is, I totally forget about it at times. Should you forget about the love within you, or find yourself in situations where you just can't seem to access it, try simply noticing, accenting the obvious, and centering yourself. If your perseverance or concentration is weak in that moment, just remind yourself that the love is still within you, and enjoy for the moment the memory of it and even the longing for it.

24

DO SERVICE

Turning your true love into action will satisfy you.

I've heard it said that someday we will all stand as brothers. I guess it's so, but until then let's not just stand around. Self-awareness is a gift, and self-reflection can boost your personal potential, but self-absorption will lead to a feeling of disgruntled emptiness. It's important to take hold of that spotlight of awareness you control and to lovingly shine it out on others as often as you can. Notice others, their wants and their needs, and offer yourself to them. The love within you is a gift you can share through action. To do so will fill you with gratification and it can benefit humankind. Help out. Regardless of how you choose to help, as long as your intention is clear, you are in touch with the love within you, and you are doing what you choose to do in a manner consistent with your experience of true love, you will feel good and others will benefit. You can deter yourself from the fulfillment inherent in doing service for others by getting caught up in concepts *about* what loving behavior looks like. Don't. Just tap into the love and let it manifest in your actions toward others. If you are faithful to the natural experience of true love within you, you will feel terrific and other people will benefit from the experience.

Service and servitude are not the same. Sacrifice is

not what makes for good deeds; loving action is. Good works are pervaded by common sense and intention, not by suffering. From my experience as a therapist and consultant, I want to emphatically announce that no single factor causes more damage and confusion in relationships than people taking excessive responsibility for one another's woes. Sometimes too much help is not helpful. A Vietnamese proverb speaks profoundly of the balance between taking care of yourself and doing service for others:

> "While it is noble to help an elephant which has been stricken, it is foolish to attempt to catch one that is falling."

I'm grateful that my profession affords me daily opportunities to do service for others. Often I'm able to do so by using and teaching the methods I've shared with you: simply noticing, accenting the obvious, playing with options, redesigning, and re-experiencing.

This morning Ruth came into my waiting room for her first visit. She was wearing a proper church-lady dress. Her hair was in a bun and her face was all scrunched up like she had smelled something awful. She prissed into my interview room. Her steps were tiny and quick and her back was rigor mortis stiff. She took a seat, placing her tiny little bottom so lightly on the couch she barely dented it. I took a seat facing her.

Ruth sat with her thighs squeezed together, her elbows close to her sides, and her hands atop her hard-backed patent leather purse. Pressing her thin lips together, she gave me a squinty-eyed tea party smile. We chit-chatted for a moment, then I asked her what was up. She hemmed and hawed for a few seconds and then told me that her husband ignored her.

I asked her if she had ever made mud-pies.

She asked me, "Will this help?"

I asked her, "Would what help?"

She said, "To talk about whether or not I've ever made mud pies."

I said I didn't know but that I thought that it might.

She looked away.

I suggested she relax her breathing and allow herself to ramble.

She said, "I just don't know," and looked down at the floor.

I leaned forward, put my head even lower than hers, and looked up at her.

She looked away and said, "I just don't know if this will do any good."

I said, "What does 'any good' mean? What would be 'good'?"

She didn't answer.

I asked again, "What would be 'good'?"

She said, "Just to be happy, I guess."

I asked her if she was unhappy.

She said, "I suppose I am."

I said, "Say 'I am unhappy'."

She said, "I am unhappy."

I said, "Say it again, and look me in the eye so that I get the message."

She looked at me and said, "I am unhappy. I am so very unhappy."

I said, "Relax your breathing and say it again."

She did. Tears came. She sobbed heavily for a long time. I took the purse from Ruth's hands and placed it beside her. She moved her hands to her face and she cried and sputtered and breathed, and cried and sputtered and breathed some more. I handed her some tissues and moved onto the couch next to her, placing my hand on her back as she heaved with sadness. After a while she mumbled through her tears, "There has to be more."

I said, "Say 'I want more.' " She did.

I said, "Say it louder."

She said, "I want more."

I said, "Clear your breathing and say it louder." She did.

I said, "Close your eyes and picture your husband and say the words to him." I asked her to notice what happened to her breathing as she pictured him. She did.

In the next forty minutes of our fifty-minute session, Ruth gave continued expression to her natural self and I think she relearned some things about responsibility, choice, feelings as energy, where she ends and other folks begin, asking for what she wants, working through conflict, simply noticing, accenting the obvious, breathing, asking for help, and that she was not her mother. She left feeling a little freer and happier, and we agreed to meet again.

Ruth was the first of many clients I met with today. I imagine they all benefited. Not because I offered profound bits of wisdom like "say it again," but because of their guts and their willingness to dive into a full-bodied experience of themselves in the "here and now" toward the goal of increased pleasure.

Experiential learning is better than intellectual learning. It goes deeper and lasts longer. It's one reason I enjoy my work. I like it too because it gives me the opportunity to use skills like simply noticing and accenting the obvious to help others settle down into the love within them. But there's more in it for me. It's a place where I've learned to *do* in accordance with the love I *feel,* and when I do so I enjoy the process as much as the outcome.

When I'm not in touch with the true love within me, the results of my work are okay, I suppose, but my feeling is more that of being a skilled robot than that of being a feeling, loving, vibrant participant in life. When I'm so caught up in the task at hand that I lose touch with the love within me, my sessions become less stimulating and I think I am less effective.

I have the choice to be and do with love, or to be and do as a robot. So do you. Experiencing the love within you takes consciousness, intention, and—I won't kid you—self-discipline. It takes effort. But you can do it and the payoff is immediate and glorious.

Allowing the love within you to manifest in actions aimed at helping others will fulfill you. You can do helpful action in whatever arena you choose. You can do helpful actions simply by being sensitive to others, being true to yourself, and being in touch with the love that is the essence of the natural you.

25

TUNE AND TONE
YOUR SOLO INSTRUMENT

You are housed in your body. Keep it well. This requires common sense and a modest amount of effort.

For five years I was a strict vegetarian. I ate no meat, red or otherwise, no eggs or animal products, and no fish. I meditated from one to two hours every day, ran three to four miles a day, and hardly cursed or spat. It made sense at the time and I am grateful for the experience. I learned something about self-discipline and managed to keep up the regimen in the face of some lusciously seductive temptations. My dive from spiritual materialism came in 1983 when I took my son, Jonah, to Tubbs Bar-B-Q Restaurant for lunch. Jonah was six then. While he gnawed on the ribs of some blessed bovine, I nibbled carrot sticks and jalapeños and chowed down on a baked potato the size of a cantaloupe. After picking the last rib clean, Jonah leaned back in his chair and took a drink of Coke. Then he licked his lips and the tips of all ten of his beautiful little metacarpals, and flashed me an Alfred E. Neuman grin. I lost it. I leapt out of my chair, ran up to the counter, and ordered a chopped beef sandwich and a beer. The floodgates came crashing down—and I'm just as close to God and what's right as ever—I think.

There have been times in my life when I've treated my body like a temple and other times when I've treated

it like an amusement park. Lately I've thought of it as sort of an amusing temple.

I appreciate and enjoy having a healthy body, so I still stay conscious enough most days to keep it, my solo instrument, fairly well tuned. I gently nudge and in some cases bellow and berate my clients into doing the same. I feel compelled to coax you as well. I don't want to sound parental, but I do hope you'll give at least a sideways glance to the following considerations:

1. Health permitting, do at least twenty minutes of cardiovascular exercise at least four times a week.
2. Consciously stretch your muscles and bend or rotate all of your joints every day.
3. Eat sensibly. Tune into your body and allow it and the love within you to dictate what, when, and how much you eat.
4. Get a sense of your personal sleep requirements and attend to them.
5. Take time every day away from your own and others' expectations.
6. Plan out each day's activities and make a list of what you want to do.
7. Don't do two of them.
8. Don't abuse alcohol or drugs (prescription or otherwise).
9. Get at least one good long belly-to-belly hug a day.
10. Weather even remotely permitting, get outside every day.
11. Do something kind for someone else every day.
12. Tell someone what's on your mind every day.
13. Ask someone what is on theirs, and sincerely listen to their response.
14. Hang out with folks you like.
15. Never get a tattoo.

26

HANG OUT

The sweet and simple truth is that feeling content and sensual, and hanging out with folks you like, not only feels better than feeling blah, blue, lonely, or distressed—it's healthier.

There's a wealth of research in the field of psycho-somatic medicine and the relatively new field of psycho-neuroimmunology supporting the idea that feeling content gives rise to chemical reactions in the body that just may charge up the immune system and help you live longer. This appears to be especially likely when good feelings are channeled to other people. Over a decade ago, Norman Cousins tapped the medical community on the shoulder and handed them a copy of his book *Anatomy of an Illness.* It contained not hocus-pocus, but well-researched data supporting his fervent opinion that his recovery from a serious, supposedly irreversible de-generation of his connective tissue had a great deal to do with his attitude. More recently folks like you and I have had our interest piqued by others like Dr. Bernie Siegel and Carl and Stephanie Simonton, who I men-tioned earlier. They've shown us that, where cancer is concerned at least, there is every reason to suspect that seeking happiness is part of the process of seeking well-ness.

The helpful effects of a good mood appear to be even greater when at least a good portion of those loving feelings inside of you are directed toward others. There is research that gives credence to the theory that those who have a greater degree of social contact have a lower death rate, and there's even some evidence that volunteer work leads to a longer life. But research or no, it's not a mystery. If you like yourself and have people in your life you care about, you are not likely to quit attending to how you look and feel and to stop exercising, or to try to hide from life by abusing drugs, alcohol, or food.

I grew up in an irrigated paradise of the Texas plains—a piece of windblown geography with earth so parched and cracked that it's been dubbed by more than one pithy poet to be the "holey" land. It's a place haunted by dusty winds where in the spring the earth and the sky are the same color. Home-grown south plains people have wild souls, free spirits, and strange ideas. Maybe it's the dust or wind or maybe it's because, as one Panhandle prince of a songwriter named Jimmie Dale Gilmore put it, "when we were in elementary school, we all got our kicks pedaling our bikes behind the DDT-fogging trucks." (They sprayed seasonally for mosquitoes and Communists.) From high school we graduated to loftier pleasures and began getting by on getting high on love, lust, and foregone conclusions.

The Round-Up Drive-In Theatre cost a dollar a carload from my childhood through my adolescence, and during that same period it showed only one movie, *Thunder Road,* over and over again and still managed to do a lucrative business. Something other than watching Robert Mitchum run from the highway patrol was going on out there. It was teenage humpo-mania. Backseat bumping, grinding, moanin', and groanin' of the most delicious sort. Those Round-Up Drive-In Saturday nights gave us the juice to make it through geometry, history, and the Junior Holidays Dance Club. We boys and girls had a clear understanding between us. We, the "stand-to-pees," and

132

they, the "squat-to-pees," had a bond between us fastened at both ends by an unspoken, undying commitment to tear off one handful of life after another and rub it all over our bodies. We had a commitment to play, including but not limited to backseat kissing, hugging, touching, squirming, and squealing with delight. If the love lives of the masses vibrated like our Saturday nights at the Round-Up Drive-In, Masters and Johnson would have to chuck it and start selling aluminum siding.

I left the high plains as a young man, expecting to find *The Land of Milk and Honey.* Instead I entered *The Dead Zone.* I bounded abruptly through life, bumping into one sorehead after another, or so it seemed, until one day it hit me that hordes of other folks in the U.S. of A. didn't seem to be having any fun at all. They had somehow grown up without learning how to hang out. Some of them had never been exposed to the idea and others seemed to think that hanging out was for kids, not for sophisticated, grown-up, responsible adults. Still others *tried* to hang out but did a lukewarm job, probably because they were trying too hard. They planned too much, I think, and gave far too much consideration to choreographing a pleasing picture of a good time rather than having one.

Hear this. All you need for a good-time hanging out is relatively good health, some free time, and someone or some people you like being around. You don't need a plan and you don't need a reason like golf, dominoes, a birthday, or even racquetball. You can create a nice backdrop and include all sorts of ancillary props and players if you like, but truth be known, hanging out is easy once you get the hang of it.

Refine your ability to hang out. Just hobnob with the pals and princesses of your existence, making definitive statements about the meaning of it all like, "I dunno," and asking heavy-duty questions like "Duyuno?" and taking walks and sockin' each other on the arm, and pinchin' each other on the ass, and playing catch, and watching the kids laugh like magpies and fight like roosters.

I'm bad with machines and I don't understand computers, but I'm great at hanging out. It's an art, and it can be learned. I currently have a handful of ladies and gentlemen in training. They are all at various levels of accomplishment and all are progressing beyond my expectations. One has potential for mastery. You too can learn and then train your friends. If you haven't started, start soon.

27

WEAR YOUR CLOTHES

In one of my stumbling runs at trying to be somebody, I instituted an all-out dress-for-success regime. It was inspired by my admiration for the natty dress-up style of a former client of mine. He's a distinguished-looking man in his later forties, well-educated, soft-spoken, wealthy by his own volition. In his silk ties, pinstriped suits, and cordovan wingtip oxford shoes, he is a striking figure. Snazzy, as my dad used to say. In his presence, clothes-wise, I felt like Gabby must have felt around Roy. I decided to dandy up.

At my first opportunity I pulled from my closet a snappy silk tie. I like ties and buy them on occasion, but I rarely wear them. Probably because, when I do, I feel like it is my first day—like I'm brand-new. But I pulled out a sharp tie and "the suit" (as my wife, Leti, calls it), and a nicely pressed white shirt, put them on, and looked in the mirror. There was no glitz. Something was still missing. Then it hit me. Anybody can wear snappy suits, ties, and shirts. The overpowering pizzazz of my client's sharp look clearly emanated from his cordovan wingtip oxford shoes. I had none. I snatched up Leti and Jonah and dragged them with me to the biggest shoe store in Dallas.

I was a man with a purpose. I was on the hunt for some cordovan wingtip oxford shoes. Success shoes.

Shiny shoes. Solid shoes. Daddy shoes. Statement shoes.

In the male shoe world, cordovan wingtip oxfords are the top bananas. The are mondo everything, but mostly they are mondo-large. Big. And they have wide, sledlike soles. They have soles with soul. They trumpet their wearer's strong character and big bucks. At least they did on my client.

This prince of presence and I have a lot in common—two arms, two legs, and one head. But I fear that is where the similarity ends. He is six feet four inches tall and strikingly handsome. I am five feet eleven inches tall and, when it comes to looks, I am, in the words of my son Jonah, "about regular." But I found the shoes and bought them and wore them into my office Monday morning.

I was self-conscious. Not whole-body self-conscious, just feet self-conscious. I felt like God had a spotlight focused on my feet, so all who came within fifteen feet of me would have the opportunity to evaluate the overall effect of my new boppers. There I was—Mister Shoes. They seemed mammoth to me. All I was sure of that day was that I wouldn't topple over. I felt like Ronald McDonald. Not a client or supervisee let me slide. Even the otherwise restrained among them offered at least a side comment—unsolicited, I might add.

"Dress-up day, Rick?"

"Got a big meeting today, Rick?"

One student of mine couldn't resist the opportunity to wink, lightly elbow me in the side, and say, "New earth pads, Big Daddy?" Another otherwise respectful therapist in one of my supervision groups interrupted a case presentation long enough to point at my feet, chortle, and blurt out, "Those feet don't belong to that person."

I still have those cordovan wingtip oxfords. They're in my closet. About once a year I put them on just to see if I fit them yet.

We talked earlier about acts. There's nothing wrong with a good act, and you can have a big time getting your act together. You can even get props to go

with your act. You can get houses, cars, and even clothes suited specifically to the embellishment of your very own preferred performance. But it's important to remember where you end and your act begins. If you get too attached to your act, you will feel bad when you perform poorly or don't win critics' acclaim. You'll be best served to select an act that is consistent with the natural you. And let me remind you once again to relax your pact to keep your act intact.

Only buy clothes that belong to you. If you're centered and into simply noticing and you stroll by them in a clothing store, they'll call to you. If they are not on somebody else's body, fondle them, then go try them on. If they feel comfortable enough to dance in (whether you ever go dancing is immaterial), go check out how you look wearing them. If you like what you see in the mirror and the image advertises what you can deliver with pleasure, they're yours. If you have the resources, buy them. If not, it's okay. There is an inexhaustible supply of your clothes; you just may have to keep strolling until they find you.

28

MOURN YOUR LOSSES

You can lose your wallet, the big game, or a loved one. It's sandpaper rough when it's the latter. There's just no doubt about it, it's hard when someone you love dies. Take dads, for instance.

When dads die they take with them suit coats warm to the touch, brusque voices, and daddy pride. They carry off with them into the hereafter answers to questions never asked, favorite ditties, shared stories, hard times unexplained, and victories unsung. They drift off leaving you holding a bag of lonelies and if-onlys. There's no getting around it. It's hard when someone you love dies.

A loving soul is a loving soul, whether it's housed in a predominately hairless body with two arms and two legs, or in one with four legs and fur. If you've had a loving relationship with another soul and that soul makes his or her leap to the Other Side, you'll have some healing to do.

If someone you love dies, mourn. Don't be shy about crying or reticent to sing their praises. Actively warm yourself with good memories, cringe at bad ones, and curse at regrets. Give your feelings the space and the time to do their thing within you. This may take days or weeks. Express your feelings verbally and in writing. Do so with a clear intention to heal yourself. Review the past but don't try to redo it.

The true love that is the essence of your being will heal your pain if you allow it to do so, but it takes time— time with your feelings. Trust the process and eventually you will arrive at a point of choice, even if only mildly or occasionally. Notice the experience of choice and of choosing. Then, with conscious self-respect, self-love, and a clear intention to feel good, experiment with reducing time spent in mourning and increasing time spent enjoying the "here and now" and in creating a fulfilling future for yourself and the living loves of your life.

Dive into your memories and your pain when you feel the need. Accept unexpected waves of sadness and anger, and work with them, not against them. Breathe. Reflect on the gifts you received from having spent time with your lost loved one. Decide to cherish the gifts, to use them, and to embellish them. Forgive your loved one for dying. This too takes time. Intend to forgive. Find the desire to let go of your loved one. Let go of him or her. Keep the good memories and wisdom you gained from your loved one's life and death.

29

A FINAL WORD

We've covered everything from love to loss. My whole-souled wish is that this book has made you more conscious of the gift of your life and of your choices about how to spend it. Writing it has done so for me. It's a review, in a way, of what I see as the basics of pleasure. I've done my level best to offer advice that goes from my heart to the heart of what matters. Like Harry's advice to me, it's all offered in the spirit of love and friendship, and I hope for you it strikes a cord of common experience and resonates with common sense.

I wish you increasing pleasure in and appreciation of your life, and I hope too that you will never get a tattoo. By the way, if you already have one, my advice: Don't get another one.

Then again, what the hell do I know?